The Book of
STOURTON CAUNDLE
HEART OF THE BLACKMORE VALE

PHILIP KNOTT

HALSGROVE

First published in Great Britain in 2001

Frontispiece photograph:
*The Author with his parents and sister, on the
front lawn of Jo Walden's cottage in 1948.
Barrow Hill Farmhouse can be seen in
the background.*

British Library Cataloguing-in-Publication Data
A CIP record for this title is available from the British Library

ISBN 1 84114 116 X

HALSGROVE
PUBLISHING, MEDIA AND DISTRIBUTION

Halsgrove House
Lower Moor Way
Tiverton, Devon EX16 6SS
Tel: 01884 243242
Fax: 01884 243325
email: sales@halsgrove.com
website: www.halsgrove.com

Printed and bound in Great Britain by Bookcraft Ltd., Midsomer Norton

*Whilst every care has been taken to ensure the accuracy of the
information contained in this book, the author disclaims responsibility
for any mistakes which may have inadvertently been included.*

FOREWORD

During January 1998 a small group of parishioners started on a two-year millennium project to research and record the 20th-century history of the village. My role in this project was to carry out the research, locate suitable photographs and other material for inclusion in the proposed film, and to write and record the commentary. By the end of that year it became apparent that the amount of information collected was more extensive than would be possible, or practicable, to include in a film commentary. The decision was made to extend the project to include the publication of a book using the same format as that for the film.

This book is an attempt to condense 100 years of village life into a compact volume of text and photographs. Hopefully it will give the reader a brief insight into the enormous changes that have taken place over the past century; the improvements in our standards of living, the changes in our working lives, and how as a community we interact with each other, both in our normal daily lives, and our social and leisure activities.

Many of the childhood memories and anecdotes have been selected from a manuscript written by my uncle Mr Frank Palmer, who has lived in the village since 1920. Following his retirement in 1979, he purchased a typewriter to record his memories from early childhood onwards, including his 44 years of service with the County Highways Department, with 25 years as a road roller driver. I am also grateful to all the other contributors of both photographs and information, who have welcomed me into their homes and shared their memories and photograph albums. Without their help in providing information and photographs, this publication would not have been possible.

Philip Knott
Hilltop, 2001

RESOURCES

Parish Meetings minute books	1897–1958
Parish Council minute books	1958–2000
School admission records	1913–1976
Slate Club minute book	1935–1948
Village Hut minute book	1920–1971
Village Hall minute book	1971–2000
Women's Institute minute book	1942–1986
Sports Club minute book	1969–2000
Knight Frank and Rutley sale catalogue	1911
Knight Frank and Rutley sale catalogue	1918
Frank Palmer's memoirs.	

Mr Blades, *Stourton Caundle: The History of a Dorset Village*

Golden Hill in the early 1950s.

Down on the bridge in the 1950s. The Bere Regis Bus Company provided a morning service to Sherborne and Yeovil, and a return service in the evening.

ACKNOWLEDGEMENTS

Many thanks go to the following who have kindly given me information, lent photographs and helped in a multitude of ways:

Frank Palmer, Enid Knott, Ruby Bealing, Annie Bealing, Doreen Ricketts, Leslie Osmond, Mary Screen, Sylvia Gould, Betty Toone, Mary Collard, Delia Lane, Father Nigel Orchard, Ben Bennett, Helen Bennett, Mervyn Caesar, David Harris and Sue Harris.

Also to the late Jo Walden who took many of the photographs included in this publication. His dedication in photographing village events and street scenes during the first half of the 20th century has left us with a remarkable visual record, and together with the extracts, taken from the written memories of Frank Palmer, has made a major contribution to this project.

The Pound in 1910. The blacksmith's forge is just visible to the far left of the picture and closed around 1900. Here the building has lost its roof. The building on the right between the thatched cottages, with the upstairs windows boarded up, was the Parish Reading Room. After the erection of the hut in 1922, Mr Jimmy Lambert used these premises for the repair of boots and shoes. Corner Cottage and Brunsells Farmhouse can be seen in the distance. The cottage partly hidden by the Pound was demolished in 1970.

Stourton Caundle, 1911

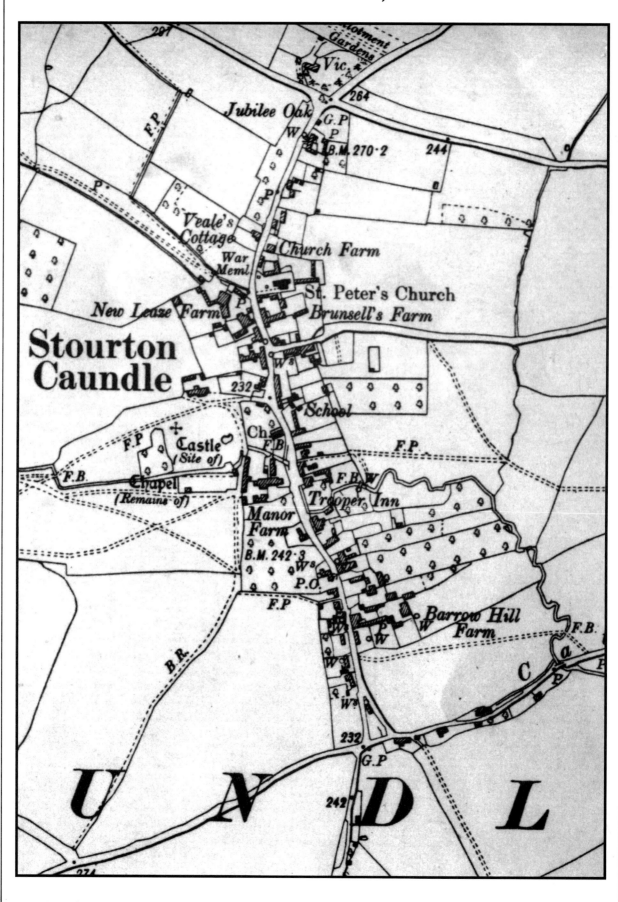

CONTENTS

The Trooper Inn and Bridge Cottages, c.1920.

Golden Hill in the 1920s.

INTRODUCTION

The history of Stourton Caundle prior to 1900 has been well researched and documented and the present volume continues from where the previous research concluded, extending the recorded history of the village through until the end of the 20th century and showing how our small community has evolved during the final century of the second millennium. The speed of change accelerated as the century progressed, with the two world wars acting as watersheds for the changes that have taken place. For the purpose of this publication, nine separate categories have been researched, the first of these being housing, which identifies the surviving pre-20th-century properties, and developments which have taken place during the course of the 1900s.

Billy Dike's bread delivery cart at Golden Hill in the 1920s.

Barley Close, formerly named Laurel Bank, was until 1935 the residence of Samuel Rice, who farmed both Newleaze and Higher Woodrow Farms.

Trooper Cottage has been sympathetically restored and modernised, losing none of its special character, and is an outstanding example of an English country cottage.

CHAPTER 1
HOUSING

The population of the parish fell from a peak of 450 in 1850 to only 234 in 1900. This was mainly due to the depression in agriculture, upon which village prosperity depended. There was a movement of inhabitants away from the parish towards the towns, to seek employment and improved living conditions. Of the 79 properties standing in 1900, 12 were unoccupied and most of the tenanted properties were in a poor state of repair, with no maintenance work being carried out on the fabric of the buildings – this was especially true of the repair or replacement of leaking thatched roofs.

Following the 1911 and 1918 estate dispersal sales, the new freeholders were also unable to afford the cost of roof repairs, resulting in the sad loss of so many thatched cottages before and after the Second World War. Others, such as Grange Cottage and the cottages at the Pound, had their leaking thatched roofs clad with corrugated, galvanised iron sheeting, as a cheaper method of preventing water penetration, and the cottage at Pophams was supported by a number of large timber buttresses to prevent it from suffering a total collapse.

There were no modern amenities such as mains water, sewerage or electricity in the early 1900s. A public telephone was not connected until 1926, electricity was not available until 1932, and mains water was not connected until 1936. The toilet, or outside lav as it was more commonly known, was in an outhouse normally located at the bottom of the garden. Water had to be drawn from a well, and cooking was by means of an iron range in the fireplace. Hot water was obtained from a copper, heated by a log fire, and situated in the wash house. The weekly washing was always done on a Monday, and a tin tub filled with hot water from the copper served as a bath. Housing policy of the Local Authority after the Second World War was to demolish the remaining thatched cottages, which had been condemned as unfit for human habitation, and replace them with Council houses, to provide a good standard of accommodation at an economic rent. Only four properties have survived with their thatched roofs intact, the front elevations on all of which have changed little during the course of the last 100 years, although all have been extensively modernised and extended.

C.1910, looking towards Golden Hill from Brimble.

Walter Hays purchased Golden Hill Cottage at the 1911 dispersal sale. He was the village baker, and the bakehouse now known as Daisy Cottage was situated directly opposite the property.

The sitting tenant, Mr James Walden, purchased Grange Cottage at the 1911 sale. He was the village carpenter, wheelwright and undertaker, with a workshop adjacent to the cottage, which has now been converted to single-storey living accommodation.

Left: *A dozen surviving properties lost their thatched roofs during the course of the 20th century. Four of these were as the direct result of fire. Sunray Cottages, formerly named Chapel Row, were destroyed by fire in April 1929.*

Right: *The residents of neighbouring properties were aroused from their sleep, amid fears that the fire would spread, especially after a large beam crashed to the floor inside the blazing building.*

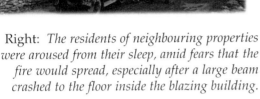

Left: *The Fire Brigade arrived from Sturminster Newton, and pumped water from Court Barton pond to fight the fire.*

Right: *Burgess, now known as Fourways, was destroyed by fire in April 1952 and the author has vivid memories from his childhood of seeing the flames leaping out of the thatched roof, towards the sky. The cottage was later rebuilt as a single-storey dwelling with a tiled roof. Planning approval was given in the summer of 2000 for the erection of a cottage on the southern side of Fourways. At the time of writing, the single-storey lean-to is due to be demolished to allow for vehicular access to the rear of both properties.*

Left: *At the time of the 1953 fire, Corner Cottage was the residence of Miss Dutton, who was the headmistress at the village primary school. It was subsequently rebuilt with a tiled roof.*

Right: *Following the 1929 fire at Chapel Row, the thatch was removed from Nos 1 and 2 Bridge Cottages.*

Melway lost its thatched roof after falling into a state of disrepair. It was to remain empty and derelict for several years but was rebuilt in the late 1950s and converted to a chalet bungalow. The thatched roof at the Dairy House (above right) was replaced with tiles in 1924, the property also being extended with the addition of the north wing. It was until 1970 the residence of the dairyman for Manor Farm.

The thatched roof at the Old Post House was replaced in 1968, the condition of the roof having declined to a point of almost total collapse due to rotten roof timbers. The Old Post House served as the shop and Post Office until 1954.

The thatched roof of the Old Vicarage was replaced in 1970. Vectis and The Rosary, both situated in Cat Lane, have also had their thatch replaced.

Another 22 properties survived the 20th century; these include Gwyers constructed in the early-17th century, and named after the Guyer family. It became an alehouse in the 19th century, and was owned by the Stokes family until its closure in 1935.

Hannsfield, named after the Hann family, was the home in the 1970s of Mr Blades, who continued the research of the ancient history of the village, and published Stourton Caundle: The History of a Dorset Village.

Berry Cottage (above) was condemned as unfit for human habitation in the mid 1930s. The cottage was saved from demolition, and renovated by the local builder Mr Frank Cook. The canopy over the front porch still survives. Veales Cottage (above right) was the residence of the gardener for Haddon Lodge. This photograph was taken in 1970 from the church tower. An extension has since been added to the southern side of the property.

The Retreat dates from the early-17th century, and was the farmhouse for Church Farm before its amalgamation with Brunsells Farm.

Brunsells Farmhouse has been the home of the Harris family for the last 100 years.

The cottage now known as Emmerdale (above left) was the residence of Mr and Mrs Ambrose Stainer. Myrtle Cottage (above right) was the residence for many years of the Priddle family. Fred Priddle milked a small herd of cows in a stall at the rear of Gwyers, following the retirement of the Stokes sisters in 1935.

The outside appearance of the farmhouse at Manor Farm changed little during the 20th century. The garden wall was removed prior to the 1911 estate sale.

Golden Hill House was the home of the local builder Frank Cook.

Walter Hays purchased the cottage pictured left and above at the 1911 sale, for a sum of £198. Hays Cottage was the home of the author's grandparents during the 1930s and '40s.

The Old Forge, formerly named Woodville, was for many years the home of Jo Walden, who took many of the photographs used in this volume.

Yew Tree Cottage was the residence for many years for Mr and Mrs Horace Parsons. Mr Parsons used a workshop opposite the cottage for the repair of domestic electrical appliances and wireless sets. Planning permission was granted in the spring of 2000 for the erection of a cottage in the garden of Yew Tree Cottage and at the time of writing construction work is in progress.

Other surviving pre-20th-century properties include Barley Cottage located to the rear of Barley Close, which was at one time the home of Miss Oliver who pumped the organ for church services. Daybrook House, a one-up, one-down cottage situated in Cat Lane, was the home of Jimmy Fritz; it has been extended recently and renamed Larkrise. The former estate cottages at Pot Knap, situated to the east of Cat Lane Bridge, and the farmhouses at both Woodrow and Higher Woodrow Farms also remain together with Haddon Lodge and Cockhill Farmhouse.

Demolished Properties

Some 18 residential properties were demolished during the 20th century; these include a thatched cottage situated in Drove Road, between Corner Cottage and where the village hall car park is now situated, and a cottage at Rowden Mill Lane where the bungalow known as Greenway now stands.

The middle section of The Cottage at the corner of Cat Lane was originally the right-hand side of a terrace of three cottages, the other two being demolished in the late 1940s.

A terrace of three cottages to the north of Berry Cottage was destroyed by fire in 1920. The gable end is visible to the north of Berry Cottage.

A terrace of four cottages together with the Reading Room, which was later used as a workshop by Jimmy Lambert for the repair of boots and shoes.

A pair of thatched cottages at the Pound, later converted to a single cottage and demolished in 1970 for the erection of a bungalow now called Anvil Cottage.

Left: *The cottage adjoining Emmerdale was destroyed in the 1929 fire and the remaining shell of the building was converted to a single-storey workshop which also served as a part-time barbers shop.*

Right: *A cottage at Golden Hill where Wagtails is now located, which was demolished in the 1930s. The boundary wall still remains.*

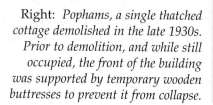

Left: *Chaldicott's shop at Golden Hill was demolished in 1936 after falling into a state of disrepair. The site was left vacant and overgrown until 1964, when R.G. Ashford & Son purchased it for the construction of Hilltop.*

Right: *Pophams, a single thatched cottage demolished in the late 1930s. Prior to demolition, and while still occupied, the front of the building was supported by temporary wooden buttresses to prevent it from collapse.*

*The two thatched cottages known as Goldsneys were condemned as unfit for human habitation
in the late 1930s. They were used as the headquarters for the Home Guard during the war years,
and demolished in 1946 to make way for a pair of Council houses.*

*Barrow Hill Farmhouse was demolished in 1963 after falling into a state
of disrepair, and remaining empty and derelict for several years.*

Non-residential properties lost during the 20th century included the village smithy at the Pound.

The Tithe Barn at Court Barton was destroyed by fire in 1964 which was caused by children playing with matches in the hay.

Downs Barton at Golden Hill, formerly known as Dowdings Barton, was demolished in 1974 for the construction of Wagtails.

Developments of the 20th Century

Only two properties were erected during the early years of the 20th century. Barrow Ridge was erected at Brunsells Knapp, and the new Rectory at Jubilee Oak was constructed in 1902, using the surplus funds from the church restoration project, completed during the same year.

In 1926 the bungalow known as Okeford View was constructed in the cider apple orchards to the north of Veales Cottage.

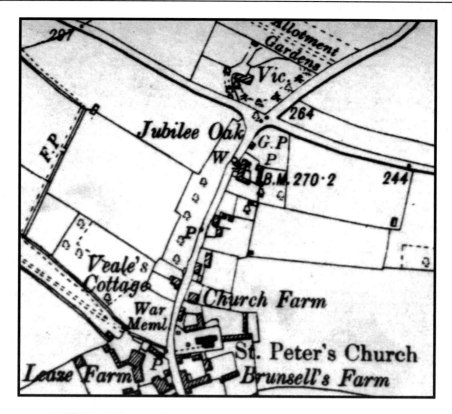

Prior to 1926, there were no properties on the western side of the road north of Veales Cottage.

Wynway was built in the mid 1930s on a plot adjoining Okeford View, and the
Little House was built in a paddock at the corner of Rowden Mill Lane.

District Council Housing Development

At a parish meeting held on 5 April 1929, a motion was passed to approach the District Council, requesting the erection of six Council houses in the parish. Land was purchased at Veales and the construction of the houses started later that year.

In the late 1930s two pairs of semi-detached houses and a block of four flats were erected on the former allotment site at Stalbridge Road.

27

In April 1942 a further approach was made to the District Council, requesting the erection of six more houses in the parish. The Council responded by letter in October 1943, indicating their proposals for post-war development in the parish. These were to utilise existing derelict sites at Pophams and Goldsneys, and provide additional sites at Sherborne Road and Rowden Mill Lane. At the next recorded parish meeting held in July 1947, plans were presented by the District Council officials for a proposed development on land at Brimble. Several alternative designs were considered and the ones felt the most suitable were selected. It was also recommended that all future properties should have a cream colour-washed exterior, and that 12 should be reserved for agricultural workers.

The first phase of the development started in 1947, and included the colour-washed properties numbered from 1 to 8, which fronted Cat Lane (below). Pophams (bottom left) and Goldsneys (bottom right) were erected at the same time, replacing demolished thatched cottages.

Nos 9 to 12 followed, and were completed in the autumn of 1948. The next phase of the development was the bungalows, numbered from 13 to 18, and the final phase of houses, numbered from 19 to 28, was completed in 1954. In addition to the Brimble development, two pairs of semi-detached houses were erected at Jubilee Oak in 1950.

Barrow Hill Close

Barrow Hill Farm in 1980. The Tithe Barn on the right-hand side of this aerial photograph lost its roof in the 1960s. The building in the centre of the picture was to be preserved and converted to a dwelling house as part of the 1990 development. A house constructed of natural stone, and of a similar design, was built on the same site.

A planning application was submitted in November 1989 for the demolition of a bungalow and redundant farm buildings at Barrow Hill to allow for the construction of eight houses. Altogether 40 parishioners attended a meeting held in March 1990 to discuss the application. The Planning Authority approved the move, subject to the re-siting of No. 1 to face the main street, and the retention and conversion of an existing barn for No. 2. This developer subsequently demolished this building. The materials used for the construction of No. 1 were to be of natural stone, recovered from the demolished farm buildings.

The developer of Barrow Hill, had also purchased the field, on the lower side of the farm yard, which was located outside of the parish settlement boundary. In the early September of 1990, an access was constructed into the field from Cat Lane. Concerned residents suspected that once the access had been established, then a planning application would follow, for the erection of a large dwelling house on the site.

On 13 September 1990 a site meeting was held at Cat Lane with representatives of the Parish, District and County Councils present, along with 30 parishioners who confronted the representatives of Fletcher Construction, the developer of the Barrow Hill site, with a petition containing 100 signatures as a means of protest regarding the destruction of an ancient hedgerow and ditch near Cat Lane Bridge. The emotive issues raised during a volatile meeting were recorded by a television camera and also reported in the local press. The District Council issued an enforcement order to close the access and restore the ditch; a retrospective planning application was refused.

Barrow Hill Close

The bungalow at Barrow Hill Farm had to be demolished before work could start on the construction of the new road into the new site.

An electricity pole also had to be re-sited.

The construction of plot 1 facing the main street on the site of the farmhouse demolished in 1963.

The materials used for the construction of the boundary walls, and also for plot one (above) were of natural stone recovered from the demolished farm buildings.

Sutton Hastoe Housing Association

In 1996 Sutton Hastoe Housing Association obtained planning permission to erect three pairs of houses on land at the far end of Brimble Cottages. The houses were to be allocated to local people at an affordable rent, to encourage the young to remain in the locality, and help preserve the age mix of the village population. The District Council had purchased the land in 1952 from Barrow Hill Farm, but this portion had remained undeveloped for the previous 44 years. Provision was made in the layout of the houses for another pair to be constructed when a need was identified, and also to avoid obstructing the main sewer, which passes through the site. A new 125mm-diameter water main was laid from the junction of Brimble Road to service the new development, replacing the smaller galvanised pipe, laid in 1947 to provide a water supply to the newly erected Council houses. The allocation policy of the Housing Association includes consultation with the Parish Council, allowing that body to pass comment on the list of prospective tenants when a house becomes vacant.

Developments by the Sutton Hastoe Housing Association.

Post-War Single-Site Development

In 1972 prior to the construction of Wagtails, the land on which it stands was the subject of a planning application by Messrs Dike and Perry, the respective owners, for the erection of 32 houses. Planning consent was refused, on the grounds that it would completely alter the character of the village.

Charterhay was built in the grounds of Fourways following the 1952 fire, and Greenway was built in 1948 on the site of a demolished cottage at Rowden Mill Lane. Vale View was built in 1974 on land attached to Golden Hill Cottage and Millway was erected on the site of the wartime searchlight station at Rowden Mill Lane. Twynham was sited in the garden of Okeford View, High Sturt in the garden of Charterhay, and Little Hayfield in the paddock at the corner of Rowden Mill Lane. Petersons Cottage was built on the site of the former builder's yard at Cat Lane, Fairways in the garden of the Rosary, and Daybrook House in the garden of Larkrise. Hilltop was built in 1964, on the vacant site at Golden Hill, following the demolition of Chaldicott's shop, the land being purchased by Mr Ron Ashford for £175. Bakery Cottage was built in the garden of Melway, and Willow Cottage at the rear of the Trooper Inn.

Post-war single-site developments include Griffin, built in 1974 in the cider apple orchard adjoining the Trooper Inn, and seen here during the May 1977 floods.

Wagtails was built in 1974 in apple orchards adjoining Golden Hill Cottage. It is pictured here after the 1994 fire which was started by a decorator using a blowtorch, which in turn caught fire to a birds nest located under the eaves. The fire spread rapidly fanned by a strong wind. Only the outside walls were left standing and all the contents were destroyed.

Hayes Cottage and Chaldicott's shop in the early 1930s.

*Greystones and No. 2 Sunray Cottages, formerly a terrace of three cottages
known as Chapel Row which was rebuilt following the 1929 fire.*

*Bridge Cottages are the only remaining agricultural workers' cottages. They were originally built
as a terrace of four, with each pair sharing a front entrance door. There was a separate door for each cottage
either side of the front porch, and separate stairways rising to the first floor from the front living rooms.*

The construction of the bridge to provide vehicular access to Willow Cottage.

CHAPTER 2

FARMING

There was a general decline in the fortunes of agriculture, upon which village prosperity depended, during the latter part of the 19th century. As previously mentioned, the population of the parish had fallen from a peak of 450 in 1851, to only 234 in 1901. Prior to the 1911 dispersal sale of the six major farms with a combined total of 1830 acres of land, most of the land and properties, including all the major farms, were still in the ownership of Stourton Estate, of Stourhead Wiltshire, the lord of the manor being Sir Henry Hoare. The rents from the farms had been little altered since 1850, due to the depression in agriculture, and the farm labourers and their families lived in poverty, working long hours for low wages, living in cramped cottages, often in a bad state of repair.

The estate's farms had been formed by the amalgamation of smaller holdings during the late-18th and early-19th centuries, together with the enclosure of the remaining medieval open fields.

The tenanted farms were held by copyhold tenure, which meant for the duration of three named lives. The low rents paid to the estate were subsidised by the payments made to the estate when a tenant died, and a new name was added to the copyhold.

The dispersal sale took place at the Digby Hotel in Sherborne, on 11 July 1911, and included all five of the main farms located within the parish boundary. Manor and Church Farms at Purse Caundle, together with Tut Hill Farm, also formed part of the sale. The total proceeds for the land and property located within the parish boundary (which included all the remaining estate-owned cottages, together with the shop and Post Office located in adjacent properties at Golden Hill) were £25 438. Manor and Barrow Hill Farms both failed to reach their reserve prices and, together with the unsold cottages, remained in the ownership of the estate until the final dispersal sale which was held on 16 June 1918 at the Assembly Rooms, Bruton.

STOURTON CAUNDLE
—— and ——
PURSE CAUNDLE
—ESTATE,—
DORSETSHIRE.
For Sale by Auction by
Messrs KNIGHT FRANK & RUTLEY,
20, HANOVER SQUARE,
LONDON, W.
1911.

35

By direction of Sir HENRY H. A. HOARE, Bart.

DORSETSHIRE,

In the centre of the BLACKMORE VALE.

7 miles from Sherborne, 12 miles from Yeovil, 5 miles from Templecombe Junction, and 3 miles from Stalbridge Station.

Particulars, Views, Plans and Conditions

AS TO THE

𝔉reehold & Sporting Agricultural Estate,

KNOWN AS

" *The Caundles,* "

Situated in the Parishes of STOURTON CAUNDLE, PURSE CAUNDLE and MARSH CAUNDLE, and extending to about

2,911 a. 3 r. 27 p.,

INCLUDING

The Greater Portion of the Village of Stourton Caundle.

To be offered in Lots by Auction by Messrs.

KNIGHT, FRANK & RUTLEY,

At the Digby Hotel, Sherborne, *on* MONDAY, JULY 10th, 1911, at 2 o'clock precisely.

Post-War Farming

Shire horses were in general use on the farms until 1940, although there was a gradual introduction of tractors during the war years, with International and Case tractors appearing at Manor Farm, and a Standard Fordson at Brunsells Farm with spiked rear wheels which required metal rims for road use. The maximum speed of these tractors was only 5mph. After 1940 horse power was rapidly superseded by the tractor. The last working horse at Manor Farm was retired in 1955.

Until the start of the Second World War all milking was done by hand. There were dairy herds at all the major farms and several smaller herds including Baker Hays at the top of Golden Hill and the Stokes sisters at Gwyers. These herds consisted mainly of Shorthorn cattle, which were introduced around 1870 and rapidly became by far the most popular breed. There was a gradual introduction of milking machines during the 1940s, but hand milking continued at Rockhill Farm until 1951. Before the war the milk was taken to either the local milk factory, owned by the Prideaux family at Gold Street, Stalbridge, or to the milk train at Stalbridge Station, for transportation to London. Most farms used horses and carts for transporting the milk, and in summertime two trips a day were required, as

there were no cooling facilities on the farms. Manor Farm and Brunsells Farm are the only former estate farms still producing milk.

After the Second World War the most common makes of tractor were the grey Fergusons at Manor Farm, and the dark-blue Fordsons at Brunsells Farm. The early 1950s saw the introduction of balers to revolutionise haymaking methods, with easier loading and transportation of the baled hay, together with barn storage eliminating the need for outside haystacks which required thatching.

The corn binders were also phased out during the same period, to be replaced with combine harvesters. The early models had a 6-foot cutting bar, with the threshed corn being bagged off into hessian sacks known as West of Englands, each weighing 2¼ hundredweight when full. The sacks of corn were then barn stored, eliminating the need for outside corn stacks, and the annual visit of the threshing team. The 1960s saw the introduction of forage harvesters for silage making, with storage of the harvested crop in a pit or clamp, the use of nitrogen fertilisers, and the practice of ploughing meadow grasslands to plant new rye grass leys also being introduced during the same period.

Post Second World War tractors gradually replaced shire horses on the local farms and implements such as mowing machines, hay rakes and corn binders, were converted for use with a tractor by removing the shafts and replacing them with tow bars.

Manor Farm

Manor Farm was known as Court Farm until 1833. The tenant at the time of the 1911 dispersal sale was a Mr George Andrews, and the annual rent for the 384 acres was £381.10s.0d. The farm failed to reach the reserve price of £7700 at the sale, and remained in the ownership of Stourton Estate, with the tenancy transferring to a Mr Adams.

A Mr William Douch from Alton Pancras purchased the farm at the final dispersal sale in 1918 and retired ten years later, at which point he handed over to his nephew Mr Charlie Garrett. Mr Douch lived to the age of 91, and is laid to rest in the village cemetery. Mr Garrett retired in 1958, and a Mrs Durrell Walters, better known as the children's novelist Enid Blyton, of Noddy and Famous Five fame, purchased the farm. During the period of her ownership, she wrote a novel entitled *Five at Finniston Farm*, and included in its storyline the rumoured existence of a gold table in a secret tunnel, linking the former castle in Court Barton with the church.

In 1964 the farm was sold to its present owner Mr Oliver Simon and substantial enhancements of the area immediately surrounding the farm have taken place during the period of his ownership. These include the creation of lakes, and extensive tree planting on the site of the old castle and moat at Court Barton. Farm workers' bungalows have been erected in the former apple orchard at the rear of the chapel, and the chapel itself was purchased following its closure in 1970. A new milking parlour, together with a self-feeding silage area, have been erected. Arable crops are grown and a store has been erected at Holt Lane for the winter storage of harvested grain. There is also a covered yard for the winter housing of dairy herd replacements, which are bred and reared on the farm. The good maintenance of highway verges fronting the farmhouse and gardens greatly enhance the beauty of the centre of the village.

The front entrance to Manor Farm.

The front elevation of Manor Farmhouse in 1911.

THE MANOR FARM

in the Parish of Stourton Caundle, containing

168a.   0r.   13p.

COMPRISING

The Old Manor House

a Stone Built and Stone Tiled Residence, pleasantly situated in the village and containing—Dining Room, Drawing Room, Kitchen, Office, Larder, Four Bedrooms, Boxroom, W.C., Two Attics, Wash House, with Pump and Well, Dairy, Cider Store, Joiner's Room, Scullery, Two Kitchen Gardens.

The Farm Buildings

chiefly Stone Built and Thatched, contain One-Stall Hackney Stable and Loose Box, Coach-House, Stable for Eight Horses, Loft over, Timber and Tiled Granary, Cider House, Barn, Cowhouse for Twenty-nine and Calf House, Implement Shed and Granary, Chaff House with Undershot Iron Water Wheel and Gear, large Barton, large Barn partly fitted for Eleven Tyings.

A Dairyman's Cottage

Stone Built and Thatched and containing Kitchen, Sitting Room, Four Bedrooms, Attic, Wash House, Coal House, an Excellent Garden.

The portion of this lot, containing 165.588 acres and forming the principal part of the Manor Farm, is held by Mr. Philip Charles Adams (with other lands) on a tenancy expiring at Lady-Day 1919 notices having been given both by the Landlord and by the Tenant.

The balance of the lot, containing in roads 5.727 acres, is in hand.

Land Tax—1s. in the £.

Price for the timber on this lot, £80 10s. 6d.

Lot 19.

(Coloured Yellow on Plan.)

THE MANOR FARM,

In the Parish of STOURTON CAUNDLE,

CONTAINING

384 a. 3 r. 19 p.

The bulk being Let to Mr. GEORGE ANDREWS, on a Yearly Ladyday Tenancy. The apportioned Rental being

Per £381 10s. annum.

The remainder, 3 a. 2 r. 4 p. of Woodland, and 8 a. 2 r. 3 p. of Roads being in hand.

The Old Manor House,

A Stone built and Tiled Residence, is pleasantly situated in the Village of Stourton Caundle, and contains Dining-room, Drawing-room, Kitchen, Office, Larder, Four Bedrooms, Bathroom, W.C., Three Attics, Wash-house, Dairy, Cider Store, Joiner's Room, Scullery, and Two Kitchen Gardens.

THE FARM BUILDINGS,

Chiefly Stone Built and Thatched, contain Three-stall Hackney Stable, Stable for Eight Horses, Root-house, Granary, Cider-house, Barn, Cow-house for Twenty-nine and Calf-house, Three Piggeries, Implement Shed and Granary, Chaff-house, Large Barton, Loose Box and Large Barn.

Also at convenient distance from the Homestead is

A DAIRYMAN'S COTTAGE,

Stone Built and Thatched and contains Kitchen, Sitting-room, Four Bedrooms, Attic, Wash-house, Coal House and an Excellent Garden.

The Tenants are under notice to quit at Ladyday, 1912.

The Purchaser of this Lot is to have a right of way for all purposes along part of the Lane No. 219, part of Lot 25, to get access to Field No. 218.

See Stipulation No. 7.

*Court Barton field in about 1970 with the newly constructed lake located
on the site of one side of the moat which surrounded the Castle.*

Chapel Barn at Manor Farm.

An aerial view of Manor Farm, 1960.

Ten years later the Tithe Barn has been destroyed by fire, and two farm workers'
bungalows constructed in the apple orchard at the rear of the chapel.

Mangold hoeing at Holt Lane in 1960. Left to right: Jim Swaffield, Ken Knott, Jim Gray, Roy Bond. In the separate picture is Eddie Bond.

Getting in the hay at Manor Farm are, left to right: Ernest Palmer, Reg Garrett, Eddie Bond.

Haymaking at Manor Farm.

Harvesting at Townsend in the 1930s with horse power. Holtham Plantation can be seen in the background, and the church tower is just visible on the horizon.

Harvesting at Townsend with Dave Bond driving the tractor and Reg Garrett operating the binder. Before the Second World War there were only two arable fields on Manor Farm – Townsend and Garvey – which were alternated each year between wheat and root crops to provide winter fodder for the cattle. The author remembers as a small boy sitting in the seat of this Case tractor unable to reach the pedals, and only being able to steer it in a straight line.

Brunsells Farm

The land attached to Brunsells Farm at the time of the 1911 estate sale included the fields located on the north-eastern side of The Wheel which were subsequently sold. The field on the north-western side of the road junction at Brunsells Knapp was the site of the lookout post for the Home Guard during the Second World War. The Home Guard members utilised the pavilion, which had been relocated to the field from the cricket ground at the rear of Veales Cottage to provide shelter. Presumably the anticipated German invasion was expected to approach the village from Waterloo Lane. In recent years a club from the Oxford area has used this field as a camping site for a six-week period every summer. The lower end of the field on the opposite side of the road junction has been identified as the possible site for the relocation of the farm away from the village centre, to enable a planned expansion of the dairy unit.

The pre-1911 tenant of Brunsells Farm, Mr Alban Harris, purchased the farm at the dispersal sale for the sum of £6300 and it has remained in the ownership of the Harris family ever since. It is currently being farmed by the fifth and sixth generations of the Harrises. The farm was amalgamated with Church Farm during the latter part of the 19th century.

There has always been a tradition of cider making at Brunsells, and both the cider house and cider press remain intact. Another feature of the farmyard is the sheet-metal-clad granary, raised on brick piers. A milking shed with a fore hay and individual ties for each cow was still in use until 1998, where the cows were chained by the neck, and remained at their allotted places until the milking session was completed. A herring-bone parlour unit, which accommodates 14 cows at a time, has now replaced this system. The farm has a beef unit and arable crops are also grown, whilst turkeys are reared for the Christmas market.

At the time of writing a planning application is being prepared for the demolition of all the farm buildings at the rear of the original farmyard, to make way for a housing development of a similar size to Barrow Hill Close. The proposed development would be outside the current settlement boundary and in close proximity to the Grade I listed church, as well as the Grade II listed Retreat, formerly the farmhouse for Church Farm, and the oldest surviving residential property in the village. An application has also been made for the erection of a milking parlour and covered yard on a green-field site at Brunsells Knapp. The two schemes are linked, in what is called in planning jargon an 'enabling scheme'. This means that the total funds raised from the sale of the development site at Brunsells Farm will be used to finance the erection of the proposed new complex at Brunsells Knapp. The intention, if the scheme goes ahead, is to increase the current dairy herd of around 55 dairy cattle to 130.

Brunsells farmhouse at the time of the 1911 Estate dispersal sale.

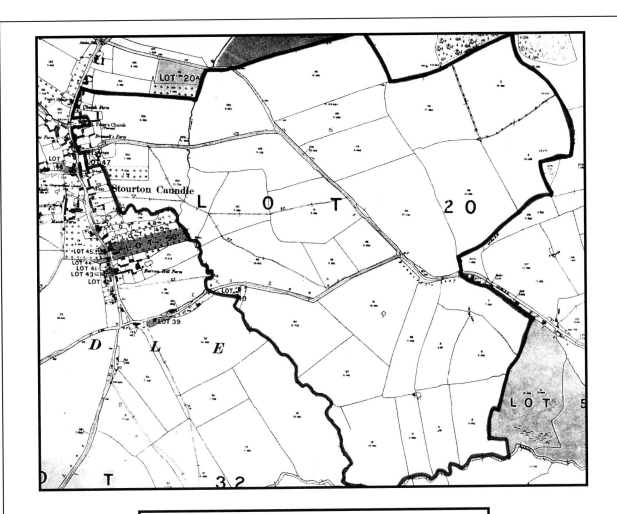

Valuable Freehold Property

KNOWN AS

THE CHURCH AND
BRUNSELL'S FARMS,

Situated in the Village of STOURTON CAUNDLE, and extending to

277 a. 2 r. 9 p.,

AND COMPRISING

A STONE BUILT AND TILED RESIDENCE,

containing Dining-room, Drawing-room, Breakfast-room, Kitchen, Dairy, Wash-house, Four Bedrooms, Cheese Room and a

Productive Garden.

THE FARM BUILDINGS,

which are Stone Built with Tiled and Thatched Roofs, are in a good state of repair and includes a Six-Stalled Cart-horse Stable, Cart Shed, Cider Store, Lumber Room, excellent accommodation for Forty-two Cows, Calf Pens, Root-house, Three Loose Boxes, Hackney Stall, Poultry House, Implement Shed, Barn and Root-house, Engine House, Four Piggeries and Boiler House, also a

Stone Built Dairyman's House,

containing Kitchen, Sitting-room, Pantry, Three Bedrooms and Two Attics, and a PRODUCTIVE GARDEN.

Held as follows :

The bulk of Church and Brunsell's Farms by Mr. ALBAN HARRIS on a Ladyday Tenancy with two years' notice, at an apportioned Yearly Rent of £287

Nos. 12, 57 and 64 by Mr. ERNEST HARRIS on a Yearly Ladyday Tenancy at an apportioned yearly Rent of 25

Making a total Rental of

Per £312 annum.

Brunsells Farm

Haymaking time at Brunsells Farm in the 1920s.

Traveller, a working Shire horse at Brunsells Farm, was sold by Alban Harris in November 1914 for the use of the Armed Forces in the First World War.

Mr Bugg at Brunsells Farm in the 1920s.

Harvest time at Brunsells Farm in the 1920s.

Newleaze / Newlands Farm

The land area attached to Newleaze Farm at the time of the 1911 Estate sale included the five fields to the north-east of Sherborne Way which now form Rockhill Farm. Also included were Newleaze Wood, and the narrow field to the front of the wood adjoining Sherborne Way, now belonging to Haddon Lodge. The first piped water supply in the parish connected a spring located in the field behind the farmhouse with the cheese-making room

The pre-1911 tenant of Newleaze Farm, Mr Samuel Rice, purchased the farm at the 1911 dispersal sale for a sum of £4200. The annual rent for the 213 acres was £193.10s.0d. Following the death of Mr Rice in 1935, the farm was sold to Mr Walter Gould, and the five fields to the north-east of Sherborne Way, to Mr Cliff Rowland. A bungalow and cow stalls were then erected at Sherborne Way, resulting in the emergence of Rockhill Farm. In 1939 Rockhill Farm was in the hands of Mr Tom Knott. The following year Mr Rowland took over the ownership of Newleaze Farm. In 1936 land at Veales was purchased from the Stokes sisters, the retiring owners of the Alehouse at Gwyers, and in 1948 a cow stall was erected on a site where the garages and a workshop are now located. In 1951 a bungalow and milking parlour were erected at Stalbridge Road, and named Newlands Farm.

Milk production ceased at Newleaze during 1963, and the farmhouse was sold as a private residence. Milk production also ceased at Newlands Farm during the same year. The Tithe Barn at Newleaze is one of the best examples of its kind left standing in the Blackmore Vale, and is now used as a potato store. The current farming activities include arable crops such as corn and potatoes, together with a flock of Sussex Border sheep crossed with Leicesters, and a beef unit. Dairy herd replacements are also reared.

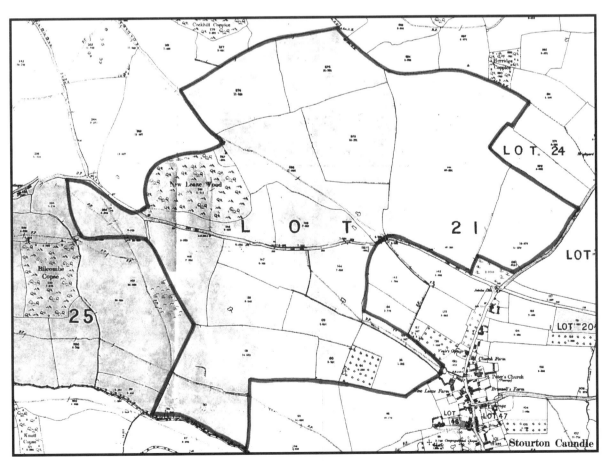

Newleaze Farm at the time of the 1911 Stourton Estate sale.

Lot 21.

(Coloured Blue on Plan.)

New Leaze Farm,

Situated in the Village of STOURTON CAUNDLE, 7 miles from Sherborne and 3 miles from Stalbridge Railway Station.

An Important Agricultural Holding,

EXTENDING TO

213 a. 1 r. 4 p.

Held as follows :—

The bulk of New Leaze Farm, by Mr. SAMUEL RICE, on a Yearly Ladyday Tenancy. The apportioned Yearly Rent being **£185**

No. 90, held by Mr. ANDREWS, on a like Tenancy, the apportioned Rent being ... ...**£8 10s.**

The Total Rental Value being

Per £193 10s. annum.

THE HOUSE,

which is Stone Built and Tiled, is in good condition and contains Kitchen, Dining-room, Sitting-room, Dairy, Larder, Cellar and Coalhouse, Four Bedrooms and Two Attics, and a good Garden.

THE FARM BUILDINGS

which are Stone Built and Tiled, comprise Granary, Coach-house, Barton, Five Loose Boxes, Cow-house for Twelve, Calves' Pen, Twelvestall Cow-house, Seven Piggeries, Seven-stall Stable, Engine House, Large Barn, Two Implement Sheds, Cow-house for Fifteen and Cowhouse for Five, Fowls' House.

THE LAND

is in a high state of cultivation, there being some Productive Arable Land and Rich Pastures.

The Tenants are under notice to quit at Ladyday, 1912.

Newleaze Farmhouse, now known as Cromwell Cottage.

The Tithe Barn at Newleaze Farm, as seen from the church tower.
The building is now used for the storage of the potato crop.

Woodrow Farm

The sitting tenant, Mr Samuel Rice, purchased Woodrow Farm at the 1911 sale for a sum of £3950. The holding had a land area of 225 acres, with an annual rent of £222. Following the death of Mr Rice in 1935 the farm was sold to a Mr Dere. Subsequent owners were Mr Weir, Mr Miles Martin, Mr Horsington and Major Peal. Following the retirement of Major Peal in 1965 the farm was sold to Col Stocker. Milk production ceased and in recent years the farm has been the location for an equestrian centre combined with a beef unit of Devon Red cattle. The farmhouse and buildings remain intact, with the roofing thatch now replaced with tiles. The current land area attached to the farm remains the same as at the time of the 1911 auction, and consists entirely of meadow grassland, untouched by a plough for the last 37 years.

Woodrow Farm House pictured at the time of the 1911 sale.
The thatched roofs have been replaced with tiles.

The farm wagons were known locally as boat wagons

A Compact Dairy Farm,

KNOWN AS

WOODROW FARM,

In the Parish of STOURTON CAUNDLE, and estimated to contain

225 a.   0 r.   21 p.

of Rich Pasture Land, capable of carrying a Large Head of Dairy Stock, being well watered, adjoining good Roads, and at the convenient distance of 3½ miles from Stalbridge Railway Station.

Held as follows :—

The bulk by Mr. SAMUEL RICE on a Yearly Ladyday Tenancy.
The apportioned Rent being **£219**

Nos. 233 and 236 are in hand. The estimated Rental Value being   ...   **3**

The total apportioned Rental being

Per £222 annum.

THERE IS

A Stone Built and Thatched Residence,

with Kitchen, Two Sitting-rooms, Three Bedrooms, Two Attics, Cheese Room, Wash-house, Coal-house, Dairy, Press House, Boiler House, Pump House and a Productive Garden.

THE FARM BUILDINGS,

chiefly Stone Built and Thatched, comprise Accommodation for Seventy-five Cows, Two Calf Pens, Two Loose Boxes, Four Piggeries, One-stall Stable, Coach-house, Cart-house and Granary.

Higher Woodrow Farm

Purchased by the sitting tenant Mrs Gillett at the 1911 sale, Higher Woodrow Farm consisted of 204 acres of land, together with a farmhouse, barn and piggeries, with an annual rent of £120. The farm was sold to a Mr Martin on Mrs Gillett's retirement, and subsequently in 1954 to a Mr Hardwick, who owned the first herd of pedigree Friesian cows in the area. In 1956 Commander Ross purchased the farm and Mr David Went was appointed Farm Manager. He continued to manage the farm until its sale to Holtwood Farms partners in 1981. Milk production ceased at this time, and the farmhouse was subsequently sold as a private residence, the land was amalgamated with Manor Farm for day-to-day operations, and is used for the growing of arable crops, including corn, peas and grass seed.

Higher Woodrow Farm,

COMPRISING AN AREA OF

204 a.   0 r.   31 p.

OF SOUND

PASTURE, ARABLE AND WOODLANDS.

Held as to nearly the whole by Mrs. GILLETT on a Yearly Ladyday Tenancy.

The apportioned Rent of this will be **£115.**

No. 175 is held by Mr. RICE with Rowden Mill Farm. The apportioned Rent being **£5,** making a total Rental of

Per £120 annum.

The Stone Built Residence

contains Entrance Hall, Sitting-room, Kitchen, Back Kitchen, Dairy, Four Bedrooms, Two Attics, and Wash-house.

The Stone Built and Thatched Buildings

comprise Large Barn, Loose Box, Two Calf Houses, Hay House, Cider Store, Granary, Chaff House, Accommodation for Twenty-four Cows, Stable for Five Horses and Harness Room, Chaff House, and Three Piggeries.

Lower Woodrow Farm

Lower Woodrow Farm was a small holding located at the southern end of Woodrow Lane adjoining the Caundle Brook. The premises consisted of a Thatched cottage, a barn and pig sties The farm had ceased to operate as a separate unit prior to the 1911 sale, with the cottage vacated and falling into a state of disrepair. Mr Samuel Rice the sitting tenant purchased the holding at the1911 estate dispersal sale, and amalgamated it with Woodrow Farm. The cottage and buildings were allowed to collapse, and by the 1920s only the foundations were still visible. Any traces of evidence that a cottage and farm buildings once stood on this site, have now completely disappeared.

A Desirable . .

SMALL HOLDING,

Situated in Woodrow Lane, in the Parish of STOURTON CAUNDLE,

CONTAINING

6 a.   1 r.   35 p.

Stone Built and Thatched Cottage,

Having Kitchen, Sitting-room, Three Bedrooms, Pantry and Wash-house, and a Good Garden.

THE FARM BUILDINGS,

Stone and Timber Built, with Thatched Roof, contain Stable, Large Barn, and Two Piggeries.

Held with Woodrow Farm on a Yearly Ladyday Tenancy.
The Apportioned Rent being

Per £10 annum.

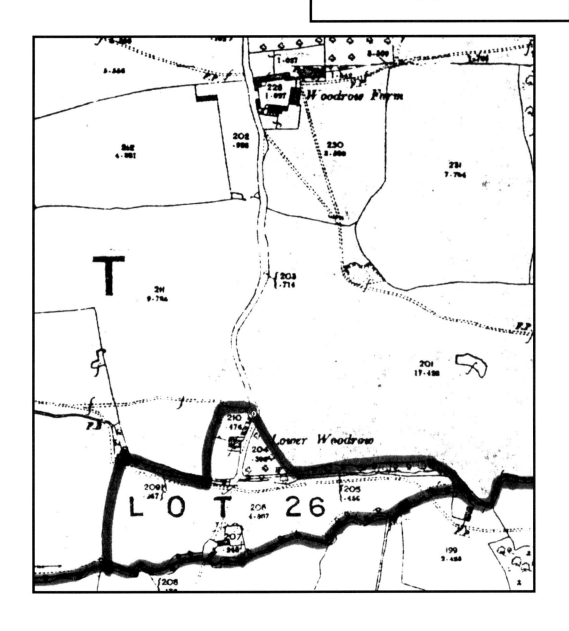

Barrow Hill Farm

Purchased by the sitting tenant Mr Ernest Harris, at the final dispersal sale in 1918, the farmhouse and house and dairy herd were rented to a Mr Harry Holdway. The renting of dairy herds was a common practice in the 19th and early-20th centuries. The farmer provided the cows, and all the food required, at the rate of approximately three acres for each cow, partly for summer grazing and partly for hay in winter, in return for an agreed rent for each cow. During the late 1950s, a large part of the land was sold to a Mr Paull of Woodbridge Farm, and milk production ceased. The farmhouse remained empty following Mr Holdway's retirement, and was eventually declared unsafe. Following a demolition order from the District Council it was knocked down in 1963.

The remaining farm buildings, including stabling and a barn, fell into a state of disrepair and were demolished in 1990 to make way for the new housing development of Barrow Hill Close (see page 29). The stone recovered from the demolished buildings was used to construct the boundary walls of the development, and also for the external walls of No. 1, which is located on the site of the former farmhouse.

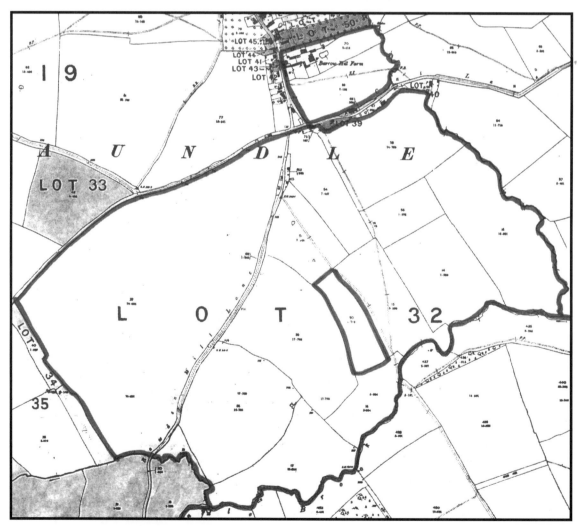

Barrow Hill Farm at the time of the 1911 sale. It was finally sold at the 1918 dispersal sale. The isolated field in the centre of the map belonged to the Trooper Inn. The large field on the left, located between Rowden Mill Lane and Caundle Lane, was called Gurt Ground. Lot 33 at the corner of Holt Lane was the former allotment site, and has been incorporated into the neighbouring field of Greenway.

Barrow Hill Farmhouse at the time of the 1911 Estate Sale

A Mixed Agricultural Holding,

KNOWN AS

BARROW HILL FARM,

Situated in the Parish of STOURTON CAUNDLE, and extending to

211 a. 1 r. 0 p.

OF

RICH GRAZING AND ARABLE LAND,

in a high state of cultivation.

Held as follows :

      The bulk of Barrow Hill Farm, by Mr. ERNEST HARRIS, on a Yearly

      Ladyday Tenancy, at the apportioned Yearly Rent of **£264**

      Nos. 17, 19 and 38 on Plan, by Mr. SAMUEL RICE, on a Yearly Ladyday

      Tenancy. The apportioned Yearly Rent being **45**

Making a Total Rental of

Per £309 annum.

Rowden Mill Farm

Rowden Mill Farm was a smallholding situated at the end of Rowden Mill Lane, which consisted of 47 acres of land, together with stone-built and thatched farm buildings, in the tenancy of Mr Samuel Rice, with an annual rent of £45. During the early 1920s, a First World War Army hut was erected near the farm buildings, to provide living accommodation for a Captain Alport, who reared pigs and kept a house cow. A Mr Martin, who had also purchased Higher Woodrow from Mrs Gillett, owned the farm. Following Major Martin's retirement in 1954 a Mr Hardwick, who had also bought Higher Woodrow, purchased the farm. It was sold again in 1956 and a brick bungalow was erected to replace the wooden building. Two fields have been sold to Manor Farm, and the remaining land and buildings are now in the ownership of Mr Cyril Young.

An Attractive

SMALL HOLDING

KNOWN AS

"ROWDEN MILL" FARM,

In the Parish of STOURTON CAUNDLE, 7 miles from Sherborne,

AND CONTAINING AN AREA OF

47 a. 0 r. 8 p.

OF

FIRST-CLASS GRAZING LAND.

Let to Mr. SAMUEL RICE, with other Lands, on a Yearly Lady-day Tenancy. The apportioned Rent being

Per £45 annum,

AND CONTAINING

Stone Built and Thatched Farm Buildings,

COMPRISING

Large Barton, Two Loose Boxes, Cow-house for Three, Pig-sty, Barn, Stable, Good Garden and Orchards.

THERE IS AN EXCELLENT WATER SUPPLY.

The Tenant is under notice to quit at Ladyday, 1912.

Rockhill Farm

Rockhill Farm was established by Mr Tom Knott in 1939, following the purchase of 65 acres of land, together with a recently erected bungalow at Sherborne Way. The land was purchased from Mr Cliff Rowland of Newleaze Farm. The farm continued as a dairy farm until the autumn of 1999, when milking discontinued. The holding is still in the ownership of the Knott family.

Caundle Farm

Caundle Farm came into being after Mr Paull bought 165 acres of land from Mr George Harris of Barrow Hill Farm during the late 1950s. A farmhouse and buildings were erected at Caundle Lane in 1960, and during that same year a major barn fire occurred in the middle of the night. Villagers were awakened by the noise of the asbestos sheets as they cracked in the fierce heat of the flames.

Despite the blaze, the farm survived and continued as a dairy holding until Mr Henry Paull's retirement in 1998. Pigs were also reared for the Marks and Spencer food stores. Milk production ceased following the purchase of the farm by T.J. Rowland Farms Ltd, and it has now been amalgamated with Newlands Farm.

Woodclose Poultry Farm

In the early 1930s a Captain Lee Evans purchased a small area of scrubland at Sherborne Way. The land was cleared for the erection of a bungalow and poultry houses, to establish Woodclose, a specialist poultry farm with the hens accommodated in deep-litter houses. Captain Lee Evans was a retired Naval officer who owned a cinematograph, and silent moving pictures were put on display in the Village Hut once a fortnight. Most of the films shown were comedies featuring such artists as Charlie Chaplin. Technical faults often caused long delays, and then there was inevitably another long delay at the interval for the film spool to be rewound. A collection (supposedly of silver) was taken during the interval, which often contained a number of metal buttons. The film shows ceased when the collections taken failed to meet the costs incurred. A Mr Raymond Foot purchased Woodclose in 1955 from a Mr Muddiman. During the 1960s the farm expanded to become one of the largest poultry and egg producing farms in the area. Recently a new purpose-built poultry unit has been erected at Caundle Lane to replace Woodclose. Raymond Foot on his retirement in 1990, passed the main business on to his nephews, who have since built a new poultry unit at Caundle Lane, delivering eggs to customers all over the south of England. Raymond Foot continues to supply eggs in the locality. He has now planted a small wood known as Woodclose copse on part of his land.

Haddon Lodge

Haddon Lodge was constructed in 1861, just within the north-west boundary of the parish adjoining Cockhill Farm, by Hugh Dalton Haskell Serrell. The Serrell family had previously lived on the western side of the road opposite the church. The land owned by the family included Cockhill Farm.

Apart from the land at Veales and Slaughterhouse Lane, owned by the Stokes family, and a single field at Rowden Mill Lane belonging to the Trooper Inn, this was the only agricultural land not in the ownership of Stourton Estate prior to the 1911 sale. In 1920, Haddon Lodge and Cockhill Farm were purchased by Mr George Fernandes, who during the period of his ownership carried out extensive and detailed research of the ancient history of the village, which made a major contribution to the book published in 1974. Due to failing health Mr Fernandes sold Haddon Lodge to Miss Doris and Miss Nancy Ludlow in 1944, and Cockhill Farm to the Inwood estate of Henstridge. Mr Dick Bennett took over the tenancy of Cockhill Farm in 1946, and Haddon Lodge became a separate farm with a herd of pedigree Ayrshire cows, a herd of pedigree Landrace pigs, and a poultry unit. Farming activities have now ceased at both locations, and the land now forms part of Stalbridge Estate.

Photograph in text: *Miss Nancy Ludlow riding side-saddle with the Merthyr Guest Hunt from the Inwood estate.*

The South facing elevation of Haddon Lodge in the spring of 1980.

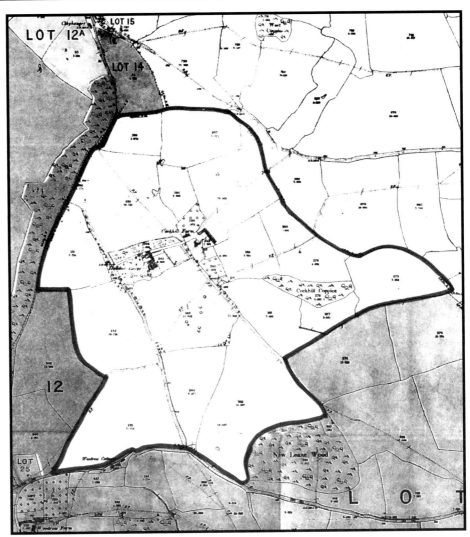

The land attached to Haddon Lodge and Cockhill Farm, and in the freehold possession of Mr Hugh Dalton Haskell Serrell prior to the 1911 Estate Sale.

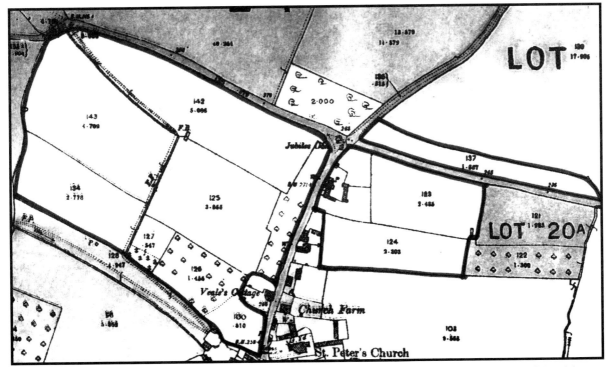

Fields and orchards at Veales, and Slaughterhouse Lane, owned by the Stokes family, the proprietors of the alehouse at Gwyers. The Stokes family continued to milk a small herd of cows in a stall at the rear of Gwyers until 1935.

Brunsells Knapp Farm

Brunsells Knapp Farm is situated just within the south-eastern boundary of the parish, at the top end of Waterloo Lane. The bulk of the land currently attached to the farm is located outside the parish boundary. During the early years of the 20th century, the Guy family lived in a cottage on the opposite side of the road to the farm buildings which was demolished in the late 1940s. A new farmhouse known locally as the Red House was constructed on a site adjoining the farm buildings prior to the start of the First World War.

William Guy owned a number of fields, located both inside and outside the parish boundary, including a field at the corner of Holt Lane, purchased at the 1918 final estate sale, and a paddock at Darkhole Corner, where High Sturt and Charterhay are now situated. Two paddocks, 'Orchard' and 'Lovells', located off Stokes Lane, still form part of Brunsell Knapp Farm.

James Guy purchased his first dairy cows in the early years of the century and carried the milk to market using a yoke and buckets. In 1939 William Guy, together with his three sons James, Vernon and George, and his stepson Frank Hollex, established an agricultural contracting business based at Brunsell Knapp Farm. After the war more land was purchased outside the parish boundary, and both the dairy unit and contracting business expanded under the stewardship of Vernon and George. The dairy herd was dispersed in 1998 in response to national changes in farming policy. Robert Guy is the fourth generation of the Guy family to have farmed at Brunsells Knapp during the 20th century, and continues to manage the contracting business.

Right: *Haymaking for Baker Hayes, at Whitemead, Brick Hill.* Left to right: *Ruby Bealing, Bob Ashford, ?, Frank Palmer, Sonny Bealing.*

Left: *The Guy family in 1920, harvesting in the former allotment field at the corner of Holt Lane opposite the site where Caundle Farm is now located. William Guy is standing (far left), next to him is his wife May, and their two eldest children Dorothy (Doss) and James (Jim) stand in front of their parents. James Guy's three daughters Olive, Estelle and Beatrice are also in the photograph.*

CHAPTER 3
ST PETER'S CHURCH

The Restoration

Major restoration work to the church started in 1899, the structural condition having declined to a point of almost total collapse due to faulty foundations and a lack of drainage and general care and maintenance. The raising of the level of the churchyard, in the latter part of the 18th century to provide more burial sites, caused the drainage problem. Under the leadership of the churchwardens Samuel Rice and Alban Harris, sufficient funds were raised, including a major contribution from the lord of the manor, Sir Henry Hoare, to meet all the restoration costs.

The work took three years to complete, and included the underpinning of the north and south walls of the nave, and the fitting of three tie beams to prevent spreading at the joints between the walls and the roof. An external concrete drainage surround was also constructed to take the water away. Other work which had to be tackled included the removal of the temporary brick buttresses, erected to prevent further movement of the walls, repair and re-glazing of the windows, the restoration of the pulpit re-sited to its present position in 1904, and the removal of the old box pews, which were replaced with beech chairs. The east wall of the chancel was underpinned, the roof was repaired, and re-glazing and redecoration were also carried out.

Further improvements to the chancel took place in 1951, as the result of a gift from the three daughters of Mr and Mrs Fernandes; these included the replacement of the ornamental screen above the altar and replacement of the choir stalls. Extensive repairs were carried out to the tower during the 1902 restoration. The belfry stage was taken down and completely rebuilt, every stone being marked and replaced in its original position. The walls and buttresses were underpinned down to the rock, and the walls were tied in at two stages with four steel rods. The bells were taken down and re-hung with a new framework free from contact with the walls of the tower, and new oak floors were provided for both the upper stages. A coal-fired central-heating boiler was also installed in an external boiler house, and connected by means of a 2-inch diameter pipe to radiators installed in the church. During the winter months, Mr Cecil Orchard lit the boiler every Saturday morning, in readiness for the Sunday services, but as it became older and less efficient, the heat it generated made very little difference to the temperature inside the church on a cold, frosty morning. Finally, in 1960, the two serving churchwardens Miss Doris Ludlow and Mr Foxwell, following visits to neighbouring churches, recommended the installation of wall-mounted radiant heaters fuelled by propane gas.

The church interior in 1900.

The church interior in 1970.

Church Clock

The original church clock situated in the middle stage of the tower was driven by weights, which required raising every 24 hours. Connected to the tenor bell, it was constructed so that it would only chime the hours, and did not have a face or hands. An iron skeleton face was erected during the 1902 restoration, but the provision of clock hands, and connection to the clock mechanism, were never completed. The clock was kept running until 1961, when due to wear and tear of the clock mechanism, and a lack of volunteers to wind it on a daily basis, it ceased to strike the hour. For the 1977 Silver Jubilee project, the clock was restored and converted to electric, the clock face was re-plated, and hands were connected to the drive mechanism. Newspapers of the time made the reports as printed below:

CHURCH CLOCK COMPLETED AFTER 250 YEARS

The villagers of Stourton Caundle last weekend witnessed the completion of a job started 250 years ago, by the local blacksmith John Biddlecombe, and the Queen has been told about it.

It was to celebrate the Queen's Silver Jubilee that the village agreed to restore and complete the church clock, it was built by the local blacksmith Mr John Biddlecombe between 1705 and 1714. The clock had never been given a pair of hands, and had stopped working in 1961. In June the Queen was informed of the project, and through her private secretary expressed great interest. The clock had been inspected, and found to be in a good state of preservation, the repairs required were estimated at £700. An iron clock face had been placed on the tower during the 1902 restoration, but hands had never been connected to it. The Jubilee committee decided that this would be rectified. After abortive attempts to detach and lower the cast iron skeleton face for cleaning and gilding, it was decided to entrust this work to professional craftsmen. Over many months volunteers carefully dismantled the clock, cleaned and painted the metalwork, and rebuilt the oak frame on which the clock stood. A specialist engineer accurately machined the escape wheel and anchor. Two motors were installed, one for rewinding the clock without stopping it, and the other to operate the striking mechanism. The hands were made from sheet brass by Mr Monk a retired engineer [and] were then placed in position on the drive spindle, by an expert in church horology working from a bosun's chair, suspended from the tower by means of ropes. The spindles and ratio gear had been obtained at nominal cost from a person in Kent, having been made for a church at Christchurch. On the completion of the project an inscription was placed in the church.

IN COMMEMORATION OF THE SILVER JUBILEE OF HER MAJESTY QUEEN ELIZABETH, 1977

The people of Stourton Caundle in the County of Dorset, through happy endeavour and willing subscription, have restored to its original sturdy form, the hour striking clock, built for the church by their own village blacksmith John Biddlecombe 250 years ago, reviving it with electric power, and adding hands for the face, which was erected in 1900. They trust that in all completeness, it may prove to be an enduring and eloquent witness of their loyalty and affection.

Churchyard

The churchyard was closed for burials in 1874, with the single exception made for Miss Doris Ludlow, who served as churchwarden from 1944 to 1961 and was buried near the west door in 1970. The two main features of the churchyard are the yew tree and the war memorial (*inset*). The war memorial is in the form of a granite cross, which was erected in 1925 bearing the names of those parishioners who lost their lives during the First World War, with the subsequent addition of those who perished in the Second World War. The Parochial Church Council

After the 1985 restoration.

served notice on the Parish Council in 1990, to absolve themselves of the responsibility for grass cutting, and the maintenance of the boundary walls. The Parish Council in turn served notice on the District Council; the result of these actions was that the District Council accepted responsibility for the maintenance of the boundary walls, but appointed the Parish Council as their agent for cutting the grass, and the general upkeep of the area. The District Council agreed to pay an indexed annual fee towards the cost of grass cutting, the sum received in 1999 being £80.

Remembrance Service to mark the Restoration of The War Memorial

The fund-raising for the restoration of the war memorial was organised by Mrs Eva Higbee (née Furnell), sister of Dennis Furnell. The surviving relatives of Stanley Haime, who was captured by the Japanese and lost his life whilst working on the Burma to Siam railway, also attended the dedication service.

Cemetery

The new cemetery in Drove Road was consecrated in 1874, on land donated by the lord of the manor Sir Henry Hoare. A dry-stone boundary was erected to enclose the area, and a flagstone path constructed to divide the cemetery into two equal halves, with wrought-iron gates at the entrance. During the 1990s, the maintenance and upkeep of the cemetery was taken over by the Parish Council, under a voluntary arrangement with the Parochial Church Council, financed from the parish precept and the income from the Fernandes Trust Fund. In the summer of 1996, a volunteer group of village residents undertook a major maintenance project. This included the removal of ivy from boundary walls, the pruning of trees, and the removal of large quantities of soil, which had accumulated against the inside of the boundary walls over the previous 120 years as the result of grave digging activities.

An extension to the cemetery was consecrated in 1978, a chain link fence having been erected to enclose the area. In 1997 the Parish Council obtained a grant for repairs to sections of the boundary wall, which were rebuilt using the same construction methods as those employed when the wall was first put in place. The Parish Council identified a Cemetery Enhancement Scheme as the millennium project for the parish, obtaining planning permission from the Salisbury Diocesan Advisory Committee. The scheme included the removal of the overgrown conifers, sited on either side of the central pathway, a tree-planting scheme, and the formation of a new access to the cemetery extension, including the erection of wrought-iron gates. The scheme was financed by a summer fund-raising event which generated £600 when a number of gardens were open to visitors including the lakes and gardens at Manor Farm, where teas were also provided. A conservation grant of £1450 was awarded by North Dorset District Council, and a generous donation of £250 given by a parishioner, all of which resulted in sufficient funding for the scheme to be completed before the start of the new millennium.

Grounds maintenance in the cemetery in the summer of 1996.

The Cemetery Enhancement Scheme in the Autumn of 1999.

Incumbents of the 20th Century

A total of 15 clergymen served as incumbents of the parish during the 20th century, most of these being only for a short duration, with three appointments in the same year in 1914. The third appointment in 1914 was Mr E.H. Fincher, and he remained in the post for a period of 26 years until his retirement in 1940. He was replaced by Mr N.E.H. Westhall who stayed throughout the period of the Second World War, leaving in 1946 to be replaced by Mr W. Delehoy. In May 1958 the Reverend S.J. Osborne, who was a master at Sherborne Boys School, came to the village. During his seven years in the post he actively encouraged the participation of the younger generation in the activities of the Church, with the formation of the Youth Club, re-forming of the choir, and for those who could not sing an introduction to campanology. Following his retirement in 1965, there was a lapse of six months before the appointment of Mr L.G. Inge. He retired in 1973, and the final appointment was Mr F.W. Summers, who came as 'Priest in Charge' for a period of two years. The parish and Purse Caundle were then amalgamated with the other Caundles, Folke and Holwell, to form the United Benefice with Mr D.J. Hillier as the rector.

LIST OF INCUMBENTS

1900	H.B. Cornwell	*Assistant Curate*
1903	S.F. Handcock	*Vicar*
1908	J.D. Warren	*Vicar*
1910	J.H. Evans	*Vicar*
1914	E.C. Hawkes	
1914	C.G. Paget	
1914.	E.H. Fincher	*Vicar*
1940	N.E.H. Westhall	*Vicar*
1946	W. Delahay	*Vicar*
1951	A.E. Barritt	*Vicar*
1954	F.L. Uppleby	*Vicar*
1958	S.J. Osborne	*Vicar*
1965	L.G. Inge	*Vicar*
1973	F.W. Summers	*Priest in charge*
1975	D.J. Hillier	*Rector*

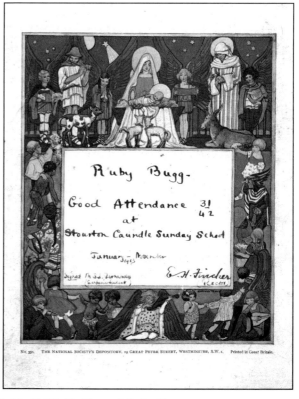

Certificates for good attendance awarded to Edith Caddy and Ruby Bugg.

Sunday School

Before the start of the Second World War most village children attended Sunday School, which was held every Sunday afternoon in the Village Hut. Religious instruction was taught by Miss Fernandes of Haddon Lodge, and later by Miss Starr, the housekeeper for the Reverend E.H. Fincher. On Easter Sunday each child was given a hard-boiled egg, the shell having been coated with a coloured dye. Every child attending Sunday School was given a stamp to stick in a book, as a record of good attendance, which would qualify for an award, usually a copy of the Holy Bible. In addition to the afternoon Sunday School, most children attended the morning service at the church, and the evening service at the chapel.

The Waifs and Strays, 1923. The Waifs and Strays was a Church-sponsored Youth Club, which met once every week at the Village Hut during the 1920s. The club leader was a Miss Starr. Games and fancy-dress competitions were organised, and each child paid a half penny to attend, the money raised being donated to Dr Barnardos. When Mr Holdway had finished milking at Barrow Hill Farm, he would play the piano for games and dancing. A Miss Young also produced religious plays to raise funds for Christian Aid.

Left to right, back: *Ivy Cook, Doris Gray, Miss Starr, Mrs Holdway, Eddy Bugg, Tom Haimes, Bert Jeanes, George Harris, Bill Honeyfield, Jack Douch, Miss Wilmott, Ernie Cook, Miss Crawford;*
3rd row: *Linda Walden, Ada Lane, Lorna Dewlian, Queenie Dewlian, Vera Foot, Ruth Mullett, Mary Honeyfield, Daisy Galpin, Evlyne Lane, Lily Galpin, Annie Jeanes;*
2nd row: *Frank Palmer, Stanley Haime, Kathleen Oliver, Bessie Stainer, Merle Watts, Amy Galpin, Lily Lane, Linda Damon, Joan Atkinson, Eileen Watts, Bessie Caddy, Eva Furnell;*
front: *Stan Foot, Ron Ashford, Nancy Damon, Marjorie Dennett, Ruby Bugg, Doris Brown.*

The Sunday School, 1932. Left to right, back: *Tom Harris, Bill Stainer, Bob Bugg, Dave Mullett, Reg Garrett, Alfred Woods, Aubrey Woods, Leslie Woods;* 3rd row: *Marjorie Lane, Enid Stainer, Ursula Walden, Ruby Bugg, Doris Brown, Eva Furnell, Kathleen Brooks, Ruth Bugg, Marjorie Dennett, Renee Andrews, Mary Brooks, Merle Watts, Noreen Chaldicott, Rose Palmer, Phylis Bugg;* 2nd row: *Gordon Woods, Dennis Jeanes, Betty Ashford, Kathleen Oliver (teacher), Ernie Cook (teacher), Miss Starr (teacher), Ivy Cook (teacher), Annie Jeanes (teacher), Elsie Furnell, Diana Walden, Vern Guy, Peter Walden, Geoff Collis;* front: *Dennis Furnell, Sonnie Brown, Edith Ashford, Jean Parsons, June Furnell, George Lane, Charlie Dennett.*

The Children's Union Club, 1941. Left to right, back: *Billy Jones, Norman Letheran, Joe Ashford, Don Orchard, Dave Mitchell, Alan Read, Eric Letheran, Robin Woods, Hubert Osmond, John Ansell, John Caesar, Revd Westhall;* 3rd row: *Mrs Mullett, Mrs A. Bealing, Mrs Bugg, Mrs Orchard, Doreen Priddle, Eileen Priddle, Rita Green, Renee Read, Vera Iverson, Stella Finch, Mrs Harris, Mrs Holdway;* 2nd row: *Harry Ansell, Barbara Gray, Doreen Green, Pam Parsons, Doll Gray, Joyce Iverson, Pat Gray, Sylvia Priddle, Marion Caesar, Margaret Gray, Muriel Priddle, David Harris;* front: *Jim Rowland, Derek Bugg, Mervyn Caesar, George Harris, Norman Bugg, Philip Antell, Don Robertson, Dorothy Ashford, Kathleen Gray, Joan Harris, Henry Finch, ?, Michael Strong.*

The 1941 membership contained a number of wartime evacuees; these included John and Harry Ansell, Norman and Eric Letheran, Alan Read, Vera and Joyce Iverson, Don Robertson and Henry Finch.

Church Fêtes

Following the appointment of the Reverend F.L. Uppleby in 1954, the annual Church Fête, organised by the Parochial Church Council, was held every summer in the Rectory gardens. During the early years of the century, village fêtes were held in Court Barton Field on Oak Apple Day. After the procession of the Friendly Society through the village and, during the 1920s and 1930s, in the orchard at the rear of the Hut, there would be attractions including skittles for a pig, and for the youths and young men of the village, a race around Wheel. The annual Fête was one of the highlights of the village social calendar; there were various stalls, children's sports and fancy-dress competitions, and teas were served from the kitchen window of the Rectory.

The format changed little from year to year, and the event provided one of the main sources of income for St Peter's Church. Support for the event declined during the 1970s, and following the benefice amalgamation, and subsequent sale of the Rectory, the annual get-together became yet another casualty of the changes in lifestyle that described the final quarter of the 20th century.

The Stokes sisters' vegetable stall at the 1922 Church Fête.

The baby show at the 1922 Church Fête. **Left to right:** *Mrs Damon, Mrs Rose Bugg, Mrs Parsons, Mrs Guy, Mrs Lane, Mrs Mary Stainer, ?, Mrs Furnell, Mrs Veryard, ?, ?.*

Fêtes

The children's fancy-dress competition at the 1922 Church Fête. Left to right: Ron Ashford, Eileen Watts, Noreen Chaldicott, ?, Merle Watts, Ruby Bugg.

The children's fancy-dress competition at the 1935 Church Fête. Left to right, back (standing): Doreen Priddle, ?, Eileen Priddle, Pam Parsons, ?, Joyce Hayward; seated: Dolly Gray, ?, Pat Gray.

The Church Fête in 1957. Left to right, back: Mrs R. Bealing, Mrs Bugg, Mrs Stainer, Mrs Ashford, Mrs Loader, Mary Guy, Revd Uppleby, Nancy Bond, Pat Gray, Mrs Padfield, Mrs Bond, Mrs R. Knott Carol Ricketts; front: Eric Bealing, Pauline Ashford, Mrs Osmond, Eva Loader, Roger Loader, Mrs Baverstock, Mrs Parsons, Lena Bond, Lesley Evans, Kathleen Knott.

Harvest Suppers

The first Harvest Supper took place in 1961 and was organised by Mr Ted Foxwell on behalf of the Parochial Church Council. The early years were notable for the home-made cider, provided by Mr Sam Harris of Brunsells Farm. The supper consisted of traditional bread, cheese, cold meats and pickles, and apple pies of numerous varieties covered with local cream, followed by music and dancing.

The Harvest Supper has proved to be one of the most enduring, and best supported of the village events, continuing without a break until the end of the 20th century. There have been slight variations in format during the intervening years; these include entertainment provided by village children, comedy sketches, a live ceilidh band with a caller for country dancing, and live and recorded music for ballroom and modern dancing. The menu has also changed to a cold meats and salad buffet, followed by a large selection of delicious desserts, all provided by village residents. Over the years the organisers have succeeded in providing a relaxed social occasion enjoyed by parishioners of all age groups.

Stourton Caundle Harvest Supper, 1961.

PLEASE COME TO THE

HARVEST SUPPER

ON

FRIDAY, 13th OCTOBER, 1989

AT

STOURTON CAUNDLE VILLAGE HALL

AT

7.30 p.m.

TICKETS:
£3.00 - ADULTS
50p - UNDER 16
FROM - ANNA OLIVER
GOLDEN HILL COTTAGE.
OR - HARRY DIKE
VEALES COTTAGE.

BAR
'GOLDEN OLDIES' MUSIC
KINDLY PRESENTED BY
PHILIP KNOTT

Church Music

Mrs Burch was the church organist and Miss Oliver pumped the organ for Sunday services, with the author as her deputy – a duty which earned the rate of 6d. per service. The position between two markers of a lead weight, suspended on a piece of string, indicated the amount of air in the organ bellows. Failure to maintain sufficient air in the bellows was immediately apparent, with a sudden change in the tune of the organ. Furious pumping of the foot pedal by the organist was required to recover the situation.

Boys, including the author, whose singing voices were not of a suitable standard to allow them to sing in the choir, were enrolled as bellringers. Mr Ted Foxwell acted as tutor, and his training provided the boys with the basic skills needed to ring a bell. They later progressed to master the art of change ringing, under the guidance of Rosemary and Helen Julius. The boys in the early 1960s bellringing group included Michael Harris, Michael Screen and Dennis Reddicliffe.

The choir and bellringers' outing to Weymouth in charabancs, 13 August 1922.

The choir, 1960. Left to right, back: Suzanne Reddicliffe, Mrs Ridgeway, Mrs Peel, Revd Osborne, Mrs Burch, Mrs Oliver, Gloria Preston; middle: Marina Shapland, Jennifer Swaffield, Janet Ashford, Jane Collard, Kathleen Knott; front: David Collard, John Foxwell, Eric Bealing.

The choir, 1963. Left to right, back: Revd Osborne, Mrs Peel;
3rd row: Kathleen Knott, Jennifer Swaffield, ?, ? Osborne (left of Revd Osborne);
2nd row: Ann Shapland, Marina Shapland, Jennifer Paine, Suzanne Reddicliffe, Maureen Else,
Ann Osborne; front: John Foxwell, Christopher Swaffield, Colin Harris, David Else, Denzil Hollex.

The wedding of George Harris and Mary Garrett, with the bride's parents, Mr and Mrs
Charlie Garrett of Manor Farm, on the left, and the bridegroom's parents,
Mr and Mrs Ernest Harris of Brunsells Farm, on the right. The best man is Sam Harris.

The wedding of Miss Fernandes of Haddon Lodge and the Reverend Asquith,
Rector of Stalbridge, who later became Bishop of Blackburn.

The Chapel

In 1859 the Congregationalists obtained a lease on a piece of land between Manor Farm and the smithy, and built a chapel. Services were held there on a regular basis, taken by ministers from Stalbridge and Henstridge. The annual service of thanksgiving for the harvest was a very special occasion. It was not unusual for the pews to be fully occupied, and for chairs to be brought in from nearby houses to provide additional seating for the congregation. Every available space was used to display the many bunches of flowers and an abundance of fresh fruit and vegetables. A loaf of bread and a sheaf of corn were placed in front of the pulpit. An auction sale of the produce would be held the following evening. Another special day in the chapel's calendar was the Good Friday bun fight, when the children would hand over a few coppers, and then wait with obvious impatience for the eating to begin. During the remainder of the evening an enthusiastic group of parishioners provided entertainment, which included readings from a book in the broadest of Dorset dialect by a Mrs Jeanes, and singing accompanied by a borrowed piano, which replaced the old harmonium normally used for Sunday services. The chapel closed in 1970, and following the 1971 fire at the Village Hut, the pews were removed to provide temporary accommodation for the Sports Club, and a changing room for the football team.

In May 2000, the chapel was the subject of a planning application by the owner, Mr Oliver Simon, for conversion to a private dwelling. The external front and side elevations, together with the windows and front entrance door, are, at the time of writing, scheduled to remain unaltered. The building is Grade II listed and situated within the conservation area.

CHAPTER 4

EDUCATION

The Village Primary School

The school building was erected and opened in 1884 as a two-class primary school; until 1929 the children's entire education took place at the school. After 1929 the 11-year-olds transferred to Stalbridge High School, except for those passing the Eleven Plus examination, who transferred to either the boys or girls grammar schools at Sherborne, providing their parents were able to meet the extra costs involved (such as the provision of school uniform). From 1958, the children transferred at the age of 11 to the new purpose-built Secondary Modern at Sturminster Newton. The secondary transfer changed again in 1974 to Sherborne, following the primary school's amalgamation with the neighbouring parish of Bishops Caundle. The school continued as an annex to Bishops Caundle until its closure in 1976, following the opening of the new Area Primary School, which combined the pupils of primary school age from the parishes of Stourton Caundle, Folke and Bishops Caundle.

In the entrance hall of the new school was placed the bell from Folke, mounted in the turret removed from the former Bishops Caundle school, and surmounted with the clock from Stourton Caundle. All of these items were stolen in a burglary at the new school building in 1982. The redundant school building, the only surviving property still in the ownership of Stourton Estate, was then purchased by the former headmaster Mr Ted Foxwell from the trustees of Hoare Estate, and converted to a domestic dwelling.

The Early Years

During the early years of the century, the headmistress at the village primary school was a Mrs Clench, and her daughter Miss Daisy Clench taught the infants class – they lived at Myrtle Cottage. In 1918 a new lady headteacher was appointed. She lodged at Brunsells Farm, and later married Mr Harry Holdway. Mrs Holdway remained as headteacher for a period of 28 years, finally to be replaced by Miss Dutton who took up residence at Corner Cottage. Miss Dutton departed after the 1953 fire which left her homeless and Mr Foxwell was then appointed as headmaster, to remain in the post until he transferred to Bishops Caundle in 1974. He took up the post as headmaster of the new Area Primary School in 1976. Miss Tite gave many years of dedicated and loyal service as teacher of the infants' class and remained in the post until the school's closure. Despite her long service, however, she does not appear in any of the school photographs. Presumably she was camera shy. Frank Palmer (*second from the left of the front row in the bottom photograph on page 77*) was the last child to complete all his education at the village school. He left in July 1927 to start work at Manor Farm, without attaining the minimum leaving age at that time of 14.

In 1884 Stourton Caundle was at the forefront of moves to bring an improvement to education in rural Dorset; illiteracy was widespread, and the recognition of the benefits of a good basic education scarcely perceived. Until the First World War all children could finish their education at the age of 11. Teachers also had to contend with truancy caused by the needs of agriculture, with children expected to undertake many of the menial tasks in the fields such as potato picking. There was strong discipline at the school, and the cane was used whenever the child's misdemeanour was considered of sufficient gravity to warrant it, with no distinction made between boys and girls.

There were four rows of double desks in the large classroom, with the youngest pupils situated in the front row, and the 10- to 11-year-olds at the back. The pupils were seated in perceived order of ability, with the brightest to the headteacher's left when facing the class, and then in descending order across the classroom to the far right. The headteacher taught a mixed age group and ability range of pupils in a single classroom without any kind of support, the children walked to the school unsupervised, and parents never set foot inside the school gate. The parents always supported punishment administered at the school.

Before the war the school playground was partitioned by means of a stone wall, and any boy caught in the girls' playground was immediately punished by caning. Following Mr Foxwell's appointment in 1953 the dividing wall was removed, morning assemblies were held in the large classroom for all of the school's pupils, and all children shared the same playtimes. Christmas nativity plays were also produced, and as the years progressed they became more ambitious, culminating in a production of Charles Dickens' *Christmas Carol*, with the Village Hall being hired on that occasion. Post-war pupils were divided into mixed age groups for outdoor activities, such as team sports and gardening. Before the war there had been no playing field, the land having been used at that time as a garden plot for the Schoolhouse. The only outdoor equipment was a swing and a sandpit, and the games played were marbles, hop scotch, skipping rope and chainey – more commonly known as tag.

In the classroom the emphasis was very much on numeracy and literacy with tables being recited on a regular basis by all the class, and left imprinted on the pupils' minds. School visits were also organised based on educational need; these included visits to the Swannery at Abbotsbury, and the Bath and West Show.

There were fewer pupils in the junior class after 1926, with the 11-year-old students transferring to Stalbridge High School to complete their education. The 1957 classes contained the largest numbers attending the school after 1926, apart from the period during the early part of the Second World War, when the numbers were boosted by the evacuees. By 1962 the number of pupils had declined, the children from the post-war baby boom having already left the school to continue their education at either the new Secondary Modern at Sturminster Newton, or one of the grammar schools at Sherborne. Numbers of pupils attending the school remained relatively consistent throughout the 1960s, fluctuating between 30 and 35.

Following the announcement of the proposed closure of the school, there was much protest and discussion. Numbers attending the school had dropped to below 30, with no prospect of any increase. The school finally closed in 1976, just eight years short of its centenary. An excellent standard of education was provided when measured against the resources available at the time, and all the pupils can look back with a sense of gratitude to all the staff who taught there.

Early Years

The primary school class of 1921. Frank Palmer is in the middle of the front row.

The primary school junior class of 1926. Left to right, back: Cleaver Walden, Bill Walden, Percy Winter, Albert Gray, Tom Caddy, Roy Lane, Eddie Bugg; 3rd row: Jack Galpin, Iris Lane, Linda Walden, ?, Daisy Galpin, Queenie Dewland, Annie Jeanes, Lorna Dewland, Eileen Watts, Bessie Stainer, Bessie Caddy; 2nd row: Meryl Watts, Dorothy Guy, ?, ? Galpin, Linda Damon, Lily Lane, Kathleen Oliver; front: Bert Jeanes, Frank Palmer, ?, ?, ?, ?, Stanley Haimes, ?.

Early Years

The primary school classes of 1933. Left to right, back: *Mrs Holdway, Jimmy Walden, Leslie Woods, Vern Guy, Mike Harris, Geoff Collis, Cliff Woods, Charlie Dennett, Miss Smith;* middle: *Vic Hayward, Dennis Jeanes, Noreen Chaldicott, Elsie Furnell, Rose Palmer, Mary Brooks, Diana Walden, Betty Ashford, Jean Parsons, Ursula Walden, George Lane, George Guy;* front: *Clifford Woods, Rita Green, Dorothy Ashford, June Furnell, Amy Galpin, ?, Queenie Hayward, ?, ?. Also present: Miss Smith's dog.*

The primary school classes of 1957. Left to right, back: *Dennis Reddicliffe, David Else, Tony Booker, Alan Bealing, Michael Screen, Roger Else, Alan Mullett, David Loader, Philip Knott, John Harris, Tom Knott, Clive Knott;* 3rd row, standing: *John Foxwell, Hilary Gray, Janet Ashford, Kathleen Knott, Marina Shapland, Maureen Mullett, Monica Toone, Shirley Booker, Ruth Bradbury, Jean Ecott, Lena Bond, Valerie Bennett, Eva Loader, Colin Harris;* 2nd row, seated: *Michael Harris, Michael Wharton, Suzanne Reddicliffe, Lesley Evans, Jane Collard, Margaret Mogg, Susan Gwinnurth, Gloria Preston, Susan Gray, Eric Bealing, Derek Caines;* front: *Malcom Gray, Danny Hollex, Pauline Bradbury, Roger Loader, Jimmy Collard, Ann Shapland, Isobel Foxwell, Carol Ricketts, Claire Ridgeway.*

Early Years

The primary school junior class of 1962. Left to right, back: John Shapland, David Hollex, Jimmy Collard, Peter Ives, Terry Brown, Tony Orchard, ?; middle: Christopher Swaffield, Malcom Gray, Colin Harris, Michael Phillips, Maureen Else, Vivian Pace, Susan Screen, Jennifer Paine, Isobel Foxwell, Denzil Hollex, Clive Knott, Roger Loader, Dennis Reddicliffe, Gregory Foxwell; front: Ann Shapland, ?, Pauline Bradbury, Ruth Phillips, Angela Phillips, Linda Woods, Wendy Richardson, Julie Reddicliffe, Helen Screen, Judith White.

The primary school classes of 1964. Left to right, back: Shane White, Stephen Shapland, Gary White, Michael Paine, Tony Orchard, David Hollex, John Shapland, Kevin White; 3rd row: Robert Guy, Linda Woods, Julie Reddicliffe, Angela Phillips, Jennifer Paine, Susan Screen, Ann Osborne, Judith White, Helen Screen, Nigel Orchard; 2nd row: Dawn Richardson, Roselyn Paine, Carol Phillips, Christine Guy, Wendy Richardson, Judith Bramble, Sandra Brown, Cherry Richardson, Linda Philips; front: Colin Chaffey, Martin Cooper, Oliver Cross, Richard Hollex, Wayne Gillam.

Early Years

The primary school classes of 1971. Left to right, back: *Robin Woods, Roger Paull, ?, Ian Jenkins, Nigel Phillips, Nick Rowland, Wayne Gillam, Christopher Brown, Vernon Brown, Mark Paull, Richard Loader;* middle: *?, Russell Woods, Jayne Harris, Sarah Orchard, Helen Morris, Jackie Duffett, Linda Woods, Tracy Priddle, Doretta Brown, Melvyn Gillam, Shaun Lane;* front: *Helen Duffett, Sharon Richardson, Yvonne Loader, Pamela Paull, Susan Duffett, Sarah Harris, Helen Jenkins, Anita Tite.*

After 1971 numbers declined even further, down to the lower twenties, resulting in 1974 in the amalgamation of the school with Bishops Caundle Primary School. Closure followed in 1976, with the opening of the new Area Primary School at Bishops Caundle. To counter opposition to the closure, the Education Authority gave all pupils of primary school age free transport to Bishops Caundle. This was later withdrawn for pupils over the age of seven, and living within two miles of the school gate. The two mile demarcation line is half way down Golden Hill.

The school nativity play, 1956.

The School Flower Show

When Mr Foxwell was appointed headmaster in 1953, he felt that the school needed some sort of corporate activity to bond children, staff and parents together, and in the summer of that year he organised the first Flower Show. At first it was intended to be a children's show, but very early on it became evident that there was a need for a full scale show under RHS rules.

In the early years competition amongst the cottage gardeners was fierce, cups were awarded to the winners of the various sections, and a cup was also presented to the person who gained most points overall. After the show, Mr Vern Guy auctioned all the unclaimed exhibits to raise money for the school funds. Various side-shows and attractions were organised, including skittles and a coconut shy. On the evening of the 1955 show, a comic football match took place in the orchard at the rear of the school between the fathers of school pupils from either end of the village, the demarcation line being the Trooper Inn. Adult sports competitions also took place in the orchard, with staggered starts for the participants in the sprint races, according to their age. The funds raised were intended to be used for the purchase of sports equipment, but such was the enthusiasm and support shown, that a 16mm cine camera and projector were purchased. In the mid 1960s a learners' swimming pool was purchased which meant that during the last five years of the school's life every leaver was awarded a proficiency badge for swimming.

In 1969 the show was jointly organised by Mr Foxwell and the Sports Club Committee. Mr Henry Paull organised a tug-of-war competition, in which teams from the village and surrounding area participated. On this occasion the money raised was divided equally between the school and the Sports Club.

The presentation of cups at the 1960 show. Left to right: Sam Burch, Ted Foxwell, Mrs Osborne, Mr New, Miss R. Julius, Ken Knott.

For the tenth Annual Flower Show, a local newspaper published the following:

10th ANNUAL FLOWER SHOW

The judges at the Stourton Caundle 10th annual flower show held last week, praised the quality of the 390 exhibits. The show raised almost £50 for the school's social and games fund. The Headmaster (Mr E.J.R. Foxwell) thanked all who had helped, and said how grateful the school was for the continued support, and encouragement it received every year.

The principal awards went to Mr K. Knott (36 points), winner of the Men's cup for the second year running. Miss R. Julius and Miss D. Ludlow (29 points each) tied for the Ladies cup. John Foxwell won the Children's cup with 13 points.

Side shows and stall organisers were Bran tub – Mrs M. Bugg. Bookstall – Mrs J. Foxwell. Pennies down the chute – Mrs P. Swaddled. Cups in basket – Mrs M. Chaplains. Cut the card – Mesdames Else, Brown and Orchard. Netball – Mrs M. Screen. Golf – Mrs L. Gray. Sweets in bottle – Hilary Gray. Pegs on line – Mrs Hollex. Quoits on stump – Miss M. Osborne. Pennies in water – Mrs C. Bradbury. Ices and minerals – Mrs M. Osmond, Mrs M. Stainer. Refreshments – Mrs Parsons, Mrs Baverstock. Gate – Mrs J. Pain. Sale – Mr V. Guy, Mrs M. Downton.

The Flower Show

Right: *Hilarity at the Flower Show. Left to right, back: Phil Antell, Ken Knott, Johnny Ricketts, Pete Bond; front: Dave Harris, David Bond.*

Left: Left to right, back: *George Harris, Vern Guy, Vern Caines, Dick Screen, Den Shapland; front: Cyril Ford, Gill Evans, Jim Gray.*

Right: *The swimming pool purchased in 1964 with funds raised from the Flower Show.*

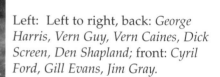

Left: *The authors Mother and Grandfather, Ernest Palmer at the 1971 School Flower Show. The coconut shy can be seen in the sandpit at the far end of the school playing field.*

CHAPTER 5

LOCAL GOVERNMENT AND PUBLIC SERVICES

Productive Arable Field

PARTLY USED AS

THE VILLAGE ALLOTMENTS,

Situated in the Parish of STOURTON CAUNDLE, and having good Road Frontage, Let with other Lands to Mr. ANDREWS, on a Yearly Ladyday Tenancy, at an apportioned Rent of

Per £10 annum,

and containing

9 a.   1 r.   19 p.

The Tenant is under notice to quit at Ladyday, 1912.

The allotment field at the junction of Holt Lane was purchased by Mr William Guy at the final dispersal sale in 1918. The tenants were given notice to quit by the Parish meeting

The tenants of the new allotments adjoining the Vicarage at Stalbridge Road in 1920.

Parish Meeting

The first session of the Parish Meeting was held on 14 December 1894. Mr Samuel Rice, who was one of the overseers of the parish, read the notice convening the meeting. Mr Hugh Dalton Haskell Serrell was elected the first Chairman. The main responsibility of the meeting was to appoint two overseers and an assistant overseer for the collection of taxes from the landowners of the parish. The assistant overseer was paid an annual salary to carry out his duties, and the revenues collected were used to help the poor and needy of the parish. These appointments had previously been made each year at the meeting of the Vestry.

The Parish Meeting was also responsible for the maintenance of public wells, the maintenance of stiles and footpaths, the provision of allotment land, and the collection of taxes from the allotment holders. Until 1920 the allotment land was located in a field at the corner of Holt Lane, opposite where Caundle Farm now stands, on land belonging to Stourton Estate. In 1913 the allotment holders were given notice to quit by Mr Adams, the tenant of Manor Farm. A letter was sent to the lord of the manor, requesting the letting of the field direct from the estate offices. The matter was finally resolved in 1915 with an agreement to rent two acres of land to the Parish Council, at an annual rent of 30 shillings as from September 1916, with a requirement for fencing to be deferred until after the end of the war. The land was allocated to seven tenants at a meeting on 4 August 1916, for a total annual rent of £4.13s.4d. payable half yearly, and a management committee was also appointed. Following the purchase of the land by a Mr Guy at the final dispersal sale, the allotment holders were once again given notice to quit, as from 29 September 1920. An offer which came from Mr Samuel Rice, the owner of Newleaze Farm, to provide 1½ acres of land at Stalbridge Road adjoining the new Rectory, at an annual rent of £4.10s.0d., was accepted by the Parish Meeting. An entrance gate was to be provided, and the annual rent was set at 7d. per perch. The allotments remained at Stalbridge Road until 1931, when the tenants were then given notice to quit by the owner Mr Walter Hays.

The Parish Meeting continued until 1958, when following local government reorganisation it was replaced by a Parish Council.

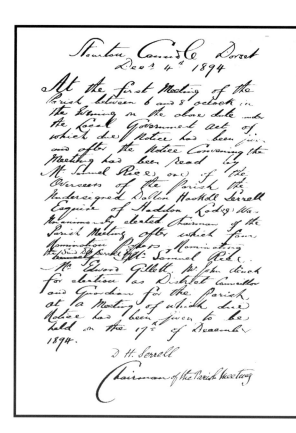

The Parish Council

The inaugural meeting of the Parish Council took place on 21 January 1958 at the schoolroom. Mr Steptoe, Clerk to the District Council, was in attendance, and presented a new minute book to the Parish Clerk Mrs Wharton. Mr Charlie Garrett was appointed the first Chairman. Items discussed at that first meeting included allotment provision, a playground, a parish map, an extension to the bus service, and a request for a fortnightly rubbish collection. At a meeting held in July of 1958, the condition of the brook outside of the Trooper Inn was discussed, the waterway having become badly choked and polluted. On 1 February 1959 an emergency meeting was held outside the Trooper Inn, with District and County Council officials present; during the previous night floodwater had reached the doors of the Trooper Inn and Bridge Cottages.

The May 1977 floods with flood water entering the Trooper Inn and Griffin. The last major flood occurred in the October of 1993 when the Fire Brigade attended to pump out the cellar and ground floor of the Trooper. A flood occurred in 1954 at the time of the laying of the main sewer through the village, and the lighted paraffin lamps, placed to protect the excavated sewer trench, floated down the High Street and into the brook. Until the late 1950s the brook contained large numbers of small fish such as minnows and sticklebacks, and one of the favourite pastimes of young children was fishing with a jam jar and a piece of string tied to the neck from the bank of the brook in Ropers Field.

STOURTON CAUNDLE
Poor Rate Assessment 1922

Allport, Charles Mathew Thomas	Yeoman	owner/occupier	£34
Clarke, Frank Bertram	Yeoman	occupiers joint	£148
Clarke, James			
Cook, Frank	Builder	owner/occupier	£22
Douch, William John	Yeoman	owner/occupier	£42
Fernandes, George	Gentleman	owner/occupier	£93
Walker, Lewis			
Guy, James	Yeoman	owner/occupier	£35
Harris, Ernest George	Yeoman	owner/occupier	£565
Hays, Walter	Baker	owner/occupier	£48
Mullett, Edwin David	Retired	owner/occupier	£20
Rice, Samuel	Yeoman	owner/occupier	£435
Stokes, Mary	Spinster }	joint	£21
Stokes, Sarah Jane	Spinster	owner/occupiers	
Walden, Josiah	Photographer	owner/occupier	£10

In 1932 the jurors for Stourton Caundle were:

Francis, Percy Harold	Newleaze Farm
Hays, Walter	Golden Hill
Walden, Josiah	Woodville
Wier, William	Woodrow Farm
Garrett, Charlie	Manor Farm } Special
Harris, Ernest George	Brunsells Farm } jurors

At a meeting in March 1960, it was reported that there was still no progress with the proposed scheme to replace the stone culverts with concrete sections in order to prevent pollution and reduce the risk of flooding outside of the Trooper Inn. The scheme was discussed again at a meeting held in December 1965. At the next meeting in April 1966, it was stated that a letter had been received from the County Surveyor, confirming that the scheme would go ahead during the then current financial year. Other matters dealt with by the Council over the past 42 years have included an extension to the cemetery in Drove Road, the provision of allotments, the provision of a play area, grass cutting in the cemetery and closed churchyard, and, in 1995, a village appraisal. A questionnaire was delivered to every household in the parish, seeking their views on subjects such as future development, housing needs, the implementation of a speed limit through the village and public service provision.

Controversial planning matters dealt with by the Council over the past 42 years have included an application for a touring caravan site at the rear of the Trooper Inn in March 1976. There was also an application for the erection of 32 houses in apple orchards at Golden Hill in 1971, as well as a proposal to erect a grain store in Court Barton Field at the rear of Barley Cottage, which was subsequently re-sited to Holt Lane, and the installation of an incinerator at the slaughterhouse. Other items discussed by the Council included the provision of street lighting; there was a proposed scheme in the summer of 1964 for the provision of 11 lights over a length of three quarters of a mile, at a cost of £25 per light. The total cost, estimated at £300, was to be financed by the District Council. The Parish Council would have been responsible for the maintenance of the lights and payment of the electricity account.

The Parish Council meets on a regular basis to consider planning applications and it is also responsible for the grass cutting in the closed churchyard, and the grass cutting, maintenance and weekly safety inspections for the play area. It provides a major contribution towards the cost of grass cutting in the cemetery at Drove Road. The Council sets an annual precept each year, and agrees a budget to finance the cost of these commitments. Planning applications considered during the year 2000 included an infill site in the garden of Yew Tree Cottage and an infill site on land adjoining Fourways. At the time of writing, an application by Mr David Harris to demolish farm buildings and erect eight houses at the rear of Brunsells Farm is scheduled to be considered by the Council.

THIS MINUTE BOOK

WAS PRESENTED

by the Members of the Sturminster Rural District Council to the Parish Council of Stourton Caundle on a Parish Council being constitued under an Order of the Dorset County Council dated the Twelfth day of November 1957 for the Parish.

At an election held on the Sixth day of January 1958 the following persons were elected members of the first Parish Council for the Parish

Norman. Else

Edward. J.R. Foxwell.

Charlie .Garrett.

Alban. S.C. Harris.

David E. Mullett

Cecil J. Orchard.

Frances. D. Wharton.

Road Building

The Rural District Council maintained the roads system in the parish until 1924, when responsibility transferred to the Dorset County Council. The stone used for road building was excavated from a quarry at Garvey, using iron bars and sledgehammers to break out the rock. The quarrymen were paid on piecework rates for every square yard of stone excavated and they were also paid a day work rate for removal of topsoil prior to commencement of quarrying. The stone was loaded by shovels into horse-drawn putts, and hauled to the location where it was required for road-building purposes. The stone was then cracked to the required size, and placed in position on the road surface for compaction by means of a steamroller.

Surface dressing of the roads did not start until the 1930s, liquid tar being forced through a lance spray by means of a hand pump requiring two men to operate it. The liquid tar was transported in barrels, which were collected by horse and cart from Stalbridge Station. During the spraying operations the barrel was hauled by a purpose-built horse putt, with a coal fire underneath to heat and emulsify the liquid tar prior to spraying. The putt was constructed with quick-release shafts, to enable quick release of the horses should the tar catch on fire. Following the tar spraying, gravel delivered from Warmwell quarry was spread by hand shovels onto the liquid surface. The weekly wage for men working on the roads during the 1930s was £1.12s.0d., with an additional allowance of 1 shilling per week, for the provision of a bicycle to ride to work.

The late 1940s saw the introduction of tarmac for use as a road surfacing material, delivered by lorry from the Mendip quarries, and dropped off in heaps along the roadway for spreading by hand shovels, and compaction by a steam roller (such as that shown in the photograph above).

Sturminster Newton District Council road workers. Left to right: ?, ?, ?, Ern Oliver, Maurice Lane, Ernest Lambert on steam roller, Bob Ashford (foreman), Ernest Winter (Saturday morning road-sweeper), Bob Green, Tom Haimes, Reg Ashford, Jim Ashford.

The men here include Mick Ashford and Billy Bugg (road roller driver).

Telephone

A telephone link to the village was installed in 1926. This consisted of two single wires, supported by a line of poles, connecting the Post Office at Golden Hill with a manual switchboard in Stalbridge Post Office. Additional lines to local farms and businesses were gradually connected in the following years.

In 1939 a new automatic exchange was commissioned at Barrow Hill, to replace the manual exchange in the Post Office. Underground ducts have been laid through the centre of the village but to date the overhead cables have not been relocated to them.

Electricity

Mains electricity arrived in the village in 1934, and to encourage residents to connect to a mains supply, the Electric Company installed three lights free of charge to every newly-connected property. Dick Meader, whose family were the proprietors of the hardware shop in Stalbridge, was employed by the Electric Company, and normally carried out the internal installation of the lighting points. Most families still relied on the built-in oven ranges for cooking, and the built-in coppers for providing hot water, clothes washing and bath water. After the war they were gradually replaced by electric cookers and water heaters.

Water Supply

A public water supply was connected to the village in 1936, the Sturminster Rural District Council having applied for a loan of £1948 under the provision of the 1875 Public Health Act, to fund the scheme for the provision of a public water supply to the parish of Stourton Caundle, and the hamlet of Stalbridge Weston.

Prior to 1936 water for all domestic purposes had to be carried by bucket from the nearest well. A number of public and private wells were located throughout the parish, including Kerr Well located in Ropers Field, with access by means of a public footpath running through the garden of No. 1 Bridge Cottages.

A 3-inch diameter cast-iron pipe was laid from a storage reservoir located at the top of Barrow Hill, Stalbridge, and constructed in 1926 to provide mains water to Stalbridge. This reservoir was supplied from a spring source at Duntish Gardens near Buckland Newton. The trench in which the pipe was laid was excavated with picks and shovels by teams of labourers supervised by a foreman who wore a bowler hat and carried a whistle. A number of standpipes were erected at strategic locations along the length of the main street, from which the residents could collect water, and these remained in use until all residential properties had been connected to a mains supply. The pipe laid in 1936 is still in use, and the parish receives its water supply from a reservoir located at Frith.

THE
PUBLIC HEALTH ACT, 1875.

CONTRIBUTORY PLACES OF
STOURTON CAUNDLE
AND STALBRIDGE

WHEREAS the Rural District Council of Sturminster have applied to the Minister of Health for sanction to borrow £1,948 for Works of Water Supply for the Contributory Places of STOURTON CAUNDLE and STALBRIDGE, and the Minister of Health has directed Inquiry into the subject-matter of such application :

NOTICE IS HEREBY GIVEN that F. H. SEABROOKE, ESQ., A. M. INST., C.E. the Inspector appointed to hold the said Inquiry will attend for that purpose at the CHURCH HUT STOURTON CAUNDLE, on FRIDAY, the TWENTY-FOURTH day of NOVEMBER, 1933, at a QUARTER-PAST TEN o'clock in the Forenoon, and will then and there be prepared to receive the evidence of any persons interested in the matter of the said Inquiry.

I. G. GIBBON,
Assistant Secretary.

Ministry of Health,
8th November, 1933.

Sewerage

A mains sewerage system was provided by Sturminster Rural District Council in 1954. Two separate lengths of pipe were installed, the first starting at Stalbridge Road and running down the length of the High Street, and a second starting at the top of Golden Hill. The pipes were laid on a falling gradient, sufficient to allow for the gravity flow of all waste products from each property connected to the main pipes. The discharge point was to be on the outlet of the treatment works, constructed at the bottom of Messlams Field, adjoining the Caundle Brook, to enable the discharge of treated effluent into the watercourse. On completion of the scheme all the earth closets were gradually replaced with flush toilets, and bathrooms with hot running water were installed to replace the tin tubs.

Rubbish Collection

Before 1936 all household rubbish that could not be burnt on the premises was taken to a local rubbish tip. There were two such tips available for this purpose, the first along the left-hand side of Rowden Mill Lane, and the second along the right-hand side of Holt Lane. The District Council introduced a monthly rubbish collection in 1936 and this was increased to a fortnightly service in 1958.

Mrs Padfield changing her library books

CHAPTER 6

TRADES

The Trooper Inn

The freehold of the Trooper Inn was purchased by Wykes Brewery of Gillingham in 1894. The first tenant was a Mr Walter Green, who also owned a pony and trap, and provided a local taxi service. One regular trip was to take Miss Serrell of Haddon Lodge to and from church on Sundays. He was also the local coal merchant, the coal being collected by horse and cart from Stalbridge Station, and stored in the yard at the rear of the Trooper.

Home-produced cider was the pub's speciality during the early years of the 20th century. The cider making would take place in the stables at the rear of the inn during the autumn evenings, with a band of willing helpers as cider making was considered to be a social occasion. There were many apple orchards in the village, and the apples were sold as a standing crop to either a cider factory or a local cider maker. The apples were knocked down from the trees with long poles and young boys were recruited to pick up the fallen fruit and load it on to horse-drawn putts for transportation back to the stable block at the rear of the inn.

Hurricane lamps were suspended from the rafters as the men built up the cheese under the press with apples and layers of straw. Pressure was applied to the cheese by screwing down the press, causing the apple juice to gush out into a wooden tub placed beneath it. The juice was then stored in wooden barrels, and left to ferment. The squeezed dry pulp that remained was known as pummy. A pint of cider cost 4d. throughout the 1930s, and the men working in the fields used to call at the back door early in the morning to purchase cider to take with them into the fields. During threshing time the threshers would call at lunchtime with their bread and cheese wrapped in a handkerchief.

Gypsy families were also regular visitors to the pub when encamped at Holt Lane; the Hughes and the Penfolds were well known gypsy families, and everyone was careful not to upset them. Sometimes they would sing and dance all night long, and there was often fighting.

General Elections were also very exciting times, with lots of discussion and argument, and customers were often bribed with free drinks to encourage them to vote for one party or the other. The games played in the pub at this time were shove hapenny, table skittles, darts and dominoes. Miss Guest's hunt met outside every season, and drinks were served to the riders. After the death of Mr Walter Green in 1928, Charlotte took over the tenancy and in the wintertime it was not unusual to see her sat in front of the open fire in the public bar plucking chickens.

Photograph in text: *Charlotte Green, landlady at the Trooper Inn from 1894 to 1948.*

The Trooper Inn Sunday evening outing, 1948.
Left to right, back: *Mrs Bugg, Mrs Green, Mrs Caesar, Marion Caesar, Burt Syblie (the bus driver), Dennis Nettley, Rita Green, Annie Bealing, Lew Gwinnurth with Sandra, Marjorie Gwinnurth, Kate Ashford, Bill Brown;*
middle: *Mrs Bugg, Mrs Priddle, Mrs Orchard, Sunny Bealing, Jean Parsons;*
front: *George Lane, Bill Bugg, Norman Bugg, Derek Bugg, Trevor Rowland, Mervyn Caesar, Paul Lane, Mr Lane, Cecil Orchard with Mary, Charlie Lake, Midge Lane, Bessie Lake;*
bottom right: *Jim Gray (drinking from bottle), Doug Lake, Mrs Lane, Mrs Caddy.*

Left to right: *Bob, Monica and Betty.*

Skittles

The conversion of the stables to a skittle alley in 1960. The author has his back to the camera.

The end-of-season Trooper skittles teams dinner in the early 1960s.

Left to right, back:
Roy Wells, Dereck Bugg, Ray Pim, Norman Bugg;
front: *Eddie Bond, Roy Bond, Cyril Bond, Syd Duffett.*

Left to right, back:
Mr Hayward, Vic Hayward, George Lovelace, Frank Palmer, Ivor Perry;
front: *Horace Parsons, Gordon Crichel, Bill Perry, Henry Paull, Bob Toone.*

Left to right: *Bill Lane, Shep Knight, Bill Brown, Jo Walden.*

Left to right: *Brian Gray, ? (standing), Bernard Gray, Adrian Bealing, Roy Bond (seated), Eric Bealing (behind seat), Brian Padfield and Cyril Bond (leaning against fence).*

Right: Gwyers, named after the Guyer family, licensed as an alehouse until 1935.

Charlotte's son Robert owned several horses and putts, which were used for road-building contracts for the District Council. He was also an expert at catching rabbits, either by ferreting or the use of wire snares. Rabbits were also hunted at night with the aid of a portable light powered by a car battery, and lurchers to catch them. Rabbits could be purchased at the back door of the Trooper for a tanner a piece. When the horses were no longer required for the road-building contracts, the stables were converted to pigsties, and pigs were also kept in the orchard between the Trooper Inn and Myrtle Cottage. Mr Green relinquished the tenancy of the Trooper in 1959 and moved to Shillingstone, where he continued working as a mobile groundsman for the County Council until he was 80 years old.

Mr Robert and Mrs Betty Toone took over the tenancy of the Trooper. The stable block was converted to a skittle alley and the interior of the pub was refurbished, including the installation of a new bar to replace the serving hatch from what is now the cellar into the public bar. The next few years were a very successful period in the pub's long history, a juke box in the lounge bar attracting the younger generation, together with darts and skittles teams attracting those not normally drawn to the inn for their social and leisure activities. Two members of the original skittles team, Henry Paull and Ivor Perry, are currently still playing at the Trooper, and Henry is intending to complete his 40th consecutive season in the year 2002.

Shep Knight and Betty Toone standing outside the front door of the Trooper in 1960.

CAMRA award in the spring of 1999.

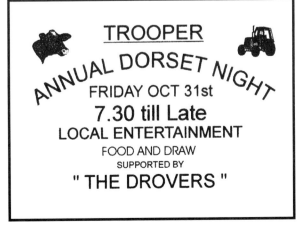

The tenancy transferred to Mr Fred Allen in 1964, and following the formation of the Sports Club and football team the Trooper continued to be the social meeting place for the village. Mr Allen left in 1971, and there were several changes in the tenancy before Mr and Mrs Dave Perris arrived in 1975. With the demise of the football team in 1975, combined with the young adults from the post-war baby boom moving away from the village to pursue careers or further education, the fortunes of the Trooper began to wane. In 1982 Hall and Woodhouse sold the freehold to Mr David Elsworth and a year later the Trooper was sold again to a Mr and Mrs Davidson. In October 1993 Larry and Sue Skeats became the new licensees of the Trooper, renting it from Mrs Davidson and subsequently purchasing the freehold. During the remaining years of the century they have managed to retain the unique character of the Trooper, as one of the few remaining traditional public houses left in the Blackmore Vale. Displays of bygone agricultural tools and other collectables are on display in the bars and skittle alley, special events have been organised, and auction sales of bygone agricultural tools and equipment have taken place.

In the summer of 1998 the skittle alley was extended to provide additional accommodation for social events such as the annual Dorset night, with the locals providing the entertainment. With the support of skittles and darts teams, and the local Young Farmers, the Trooper provides a friendly relaxed atmosphere, enjoyed by all its customers. The long-term future remains uncertain, but Larry and Sue's stewardship will ensure that the Trooper prospers well into the new millennium.

Landlord Larry Skeats building the extension to the skittle alley in 1998.

The Sunday lunch break for Dorset Vintage Motorcycle Club in the summer of 2000.

The Village Shop

Main shop and Post Office, c.1930s.

The main village shop and Post Office was located at the top of Golden Hill in the property now known as the Old Post House. The shop premises were divided into two sections, with the grocery business located in a room to the right of the entrance doorway. There were some tinned foods and jars on the shelves, but most of the provisions were delivered to the shop in bulk, and were weighed up to the customer's requirements. Foodstuffs such as lentils, rice and dried fruit were delivered in wooden chests, and tea came in three-ply chests. A small room to the rear of the grocery section served as a store for such items as a barrel of malt vinegar, and 7lb-tins of corned beef, which was sliced with a sharp carving knife. Cheese was cut with a wire and metal scoops were used to weigh up other items such as rice, which were then placed in a brown paper bag. The small centre room just inside the entrance door served as the Post Office, and boots, clothes and stationery were also stored here. Jars of sweets were displayed on a shelf in the window, in a prominent position so as to attract the attention of the children. The normal price of toffees and boiled sweets was 1d. an ounce, and better quality sweets were 6d. per quarter. As far as the small children were concerned the best buy of all came when the jar was almost empty. The child could expect to be served a large bag, full of misshapen sweets, and all for only a copper.

Empty containers from the shop were always put to good use; the orange boxes were in demand for use as nesting boxes in hen houses, while tea chests were suitable for winter storage of potatoes. In 1926 a public telephone was installed in the room to the right-hand side of the entrance door which meant that there was no privacy for the person making the call.

In 1954, the retiring owners Mr and Mrs Collis sold the shop to Dike and Sons of Stalbridge. The business was then transferred to the refurbished bakehouse on the opposite side of the road. All the children of the first day's customers were given ice creams. Mrs Margaret Downton was the shop manageress from 1957 to 1981 (when she retired) and the shop was then sold to Mr and Mrs Braun. A continual decline in the number of customers throughout the 1980s resulted in the shop's closure in 1991.

Chaldicott's shop at Golden Hill

1906

1911

The Reversion to the Freehold of

A Desirable Cottage and Garden

KNOWN AS

THE POST OFFICE,

In the Village of STOURTON CAUNDLE,

comprising Kitchen, Sitting-room, Scullery, Wash-house, and Five Bedrooms.

———

Held by SAMUEL HARRIS for the life of CHARLOTTE LYNE, aged 55, at the Reserved Rent of 1s.

The estimated value being

Per £15 annum,

The whole estimated to contain

0 a.   0 r.   30 p.

The Reversion to the Freehold of

A Valuable Cottage,

Situated in the Village of STOURTON CAUNDLE, and known as

THE SHOP,

ESTIMATED TO CONTAIN, WITH GARDEN,

0 a.   0 r.   25 p.

Estimated Value

Per £12 annum.

Held by ANDREW CROCKER for the lives of ANDREW CROCKER, aged 69, MARY ANN CROCKER, aged 58, and CHARLES CROCKER, aged 33. The Cottage comprises Kitchen, Sitting-room, Shop, Scullery, and Four Bedrooms. Excellent Garden and Piggery.

Reserved Rent 1s. a Year.

1932

*The former bakehouse, converted to a shop in 1954,
and now known as Daisy Cottage.*

The Bakers

During the 1920s three bakers delivered bread to the village. The bread was delivered by horse and cart, and the cart was fitted with a fixed semi-cylindrical canvas tilt, on the sides of which were displayed in bold lettering the owner's name and his trade. The delivery men worked from dawn to dusk on their long rural rounds, and the horses became so familiar with the routes that they could retrace their steps home without any guidance from the driver, who was often sat dozing in the seat. The local bakery was situated at the top of Golden Hill, in the property now known as Daisy Cottage. The proprietor was Mr Walter Hays and at the bakery large cakes were made by Mrs Hays, among them seed, dough, powder and lardy cakes, which were sold at a price of 9d. each. When a dozen buns were purchased 13 buns were handed over – this was known as the Baker's Dozen. The baker seldom had to resort to throwing stale buns into the pig's swill, as they could usually be sold off at reduced prices. At the weekends local residents could take their joints of meat to the bakehouse, to roast for a cost of 1d., and kneaded dough could be purchased for pastry making.

Baker Hays with his delivery cart. The left-hand side of his jacket is sagging due to the weight of the loose change in his pocket.

Billy Orchard delivering bread for Dikes Bakery.

Delivery Men

Mr Alec Roberts delivered the post to the village from Stalbridge Post Office, riding a bicycle. The delivery round started at Stalbridge Weston, and from there he pushed his cycle along the footpath to Haddon Lodge, where he stopped for a coffee break. After delivering to Woodrow, he then rode down Sherborne Way to commence delivery through the village High Street, collecting the outward-going mail from the Post Office on the return journey to Stalbridge.

Arthur Ratley owned a bakehouse in Stalbridge High Street, and delivered bread to the village by horse and cart. There was keen competition for bread sales, for as well as the local baker Mr Hays, Billy Dike from Stalbridge also delivered bread to the village. When a new family moved into the village the various roundsmen were queued up awaiting their arrival,

The postman Alec Roberts outside the Post Office.

hoping to gain another customer. On Saturdays the roundsmen worked late into the night completing their long rural rounds, having been hindered by numerous social stops along the way. Herby Parsons from Stalbridge delivered fish including bloaters, which were smoked on an open fire. Harry Kendall from Marnhull sold pots and pans and other household items, such as paraffin for cooking stoves and heaters. The Stalbridge butchers Fred Bugg and Mr Eavis also delivered to the village. The meat was fatty and tough, and the hygiene poor when compared with today's standards. At the time of writing the only roundsmen delivering to the village are Mr Dick Curtis with the weekly fish round, and a milkman who delivers milk and other dairy produce four times a week.

Travelling Salesmen

The ringing of a loud bell would herald the arrival of a travelling bazaar from Wimborne Minster. The motor van was large, and carrying capacity was increased by the fitting of an external wooden framework to both sides of the vehicle, in which were carried racks of crockery packed in straw. Earthenware pots were hung by the handle from hooks along the rows of shelves. The salesman would use a u-shaped attachment on the end of a pole for lifting down such items as buckets and large jugs. A rail was fitted to the roof for the storage of a small stock of much larger items. Access to the roof area was by means of a vertically fixed ladder on the side of the vehicle. The interior of the van was crammed full with an assortment of merchandise.

Old Jack worked from dawn to dusk as a peddler selling from door to door and made his living by selling reels of cotton thread, skeins of wool, and sewing needles from a tray suspended from his neck by a leather strap. During the 1920s, a copy of *Old Moores Almanac* could be purchased from a man who arrived in the village towards the end of

every year. He would flit from door to door, and then make a hurried departure from the village in time to catch the last train from Stalbridge Station. Gypsies were often encamped at Holt Lane and the men were usually involved in horse dealing, making wooden pegs and the shaping of bits of stick into artificial flowers for the womenfolk to sell on the doorstep.

The gypsy women were never at a loss for words and always had a tale of woe, especially if they were trying to persuade someone to buy, or begging for such items as cast-off clothing. The peace was often shattered on summer Sundays by a group of noisy men selling Weymouth mackerel at very competitive prices. Customers went to the back of the lorry with a china plate, and would inspect the fish before purchase to make sure they were still relatively fresh after several hours in transit. A man travelled to the village from Shaftesbury on a bicycle, to which was attached a workbench for the sharpening of knives, scissors and shears. He would operate the contraption by setting the bike on its stand, and using the pedals to turn the grindstone by means of belts and pulleys. Another regular visitor to the village was the horse-drawn knackers cart, a vehicle used for the transportation of dead sheep and cattle to the dog kennels at Inwood where they were fed to the foxhounds.

One man and his donkey cart came to the village on a regular basis and collected rags in exchange for bloaters; at lunchtimes the donkey and cart would be seen outside of the Trooper Inn. Three coal merchants delivered to the village and one coalman would return home with a cartload of hazel sticks bought from a local farmer. These sticks were later sold 40 to the bundle for sticking runner beans and peas. Two men sold paraffin for heating and lighting and they also sold household cleaning materials and were known to everyone as the oil men.

In 1940 Cliff Rowland erected a slaughterhouse at Stokes Lane for the slaughter of sick animals which were unfit to enter the human food chain. During the war years the slaughtermen were Cyril Knott and George Lane. In wintertime during the hours of darkness, they worked by the light of two candles as there was no electricity connected to the building. The carcasses were sprayed with green paint to identify that they were unfit for human consumption. They were then loaded on to a lorry for transportation to a retail outlet at Poole, to be sold as dog meat.

The slaughterhouse was subsequently sold to a Mr John Burden, with Mr Dennett working as the slaughterman throughout the period of his ownership, until the closure of the premises in 1998. At the height of the BSE crisis in the 1990s, an unsuccessful planning application was made to the Local Planning Authority for the installation of an incinerator to dispose of cattle affected by the disease. Local residents objected to the proposed scheme, and expressed their concerns over the smell and increased lorry traffic. Following closure the site of the slaughterhouse has remained derelict, awaiting a new owner. The original winch installed in 1940 for raising the slaughtered animals can still be seen in the yard.

The smithy at Bishops Caundle. The local smithy ceased trading around 1900.

The Smithy pictured after closure and falling into a state of disrepair

CHAPTER 7

SOCIAL AND LEISURE ACTIVITIES

All hands on deck for the erection of the Village Hut in 1920.

The Village Hut

The Village Hut was a timber-framed, corrugated-iron Army hut. Following its purchase in 1920, it was dismantled and transported from Salisbury Plain. The building was then erected on land at Drove Road, donated by Mr Albin Harris of Brunsells Farm. The incumbents and churchwardens were appointed as trustees, and together with Mr Albin Harris formed an Executive Committee, with the powers to veto any propositions made by the Hut Management Committee. The facility was to be used for the spiritual needs of the parish.

During the 1930s and '40s many happy winter evenings were spent by parishioners at the Village Hut, where they would gather for social evenings which included games, musical chairs, and dancing to the local dance band known as the Big Four. The members of the band were Harry Holdway on piano, Ambrose Stainer on cornet, Jack Senior on violin and saxophone, and George Harris on drums. The dances were the quickstep, foxtrot and waltz, and there were also novelty dances including the palais glide and hokey cokey – 'Ladies excuse me' and the 'Paul Jones' were also popular. There was much excitement and anticipation on nearing the building and hearing the music from the band.

There was a break for refreshments during the evening, and paraffin stoves were used for heating. The young single lads arrived towards the end of the evening usually after closing time at the Trooper Inn, and they tended to congregate at one end of the hut, until the first one plucked up enough courage to ask one of the girls for a dance. The others then followed, and the girls who had waited patiently to be asked hoped they would not end up as wallflowers. The last waltz came all too soon, danced to the tune of 'Who's Taking You Home Tonight?'

In 1938 another local dance band named the Bing Boys Band was formed, the band members being Bill Allen on piano, Aubrey Walden on piano accordion, Bill Stainer on trumpet, Frank Palmer on saxophone and Harold Lane on drums. The band's uniform consisted of emerald-green trousers, with a dark green stripe running the full length of each leg, and shirts of pale green. The cuffs, collars and neckties matched the dark green colour of the waistbands, and an embroidered badge of three Bs was sewn to the left breast pocket of the shirts. As well as providing the music for the Stourton Caundle hops, the band also travelled to other villages throughout the Blackmore Vale.

The 1954 children's Christmas party.

Mrs Argylle's rug-making class of 1955.
Left to right, back row: *Nancy Bond, Mick Ashford, Tony Hayward, Mrs Argylle, David Ford, Basil Beardsmore, Mary Gray;* third row: *Roy Bond, Bernard Gray, David Lacey, Geoffrey Reddicliffe, Vernon Caines, Brian Padfield, Cyril Bond, Michael Ford;* second row: *Sandra Gwinnurth, Brenda Gray, Mary Orchard, Susan Gray, Lena Bond, John Ford, Christopher Lacey, John Harris, Monica Toone, Lesley Evans;* front row: *Heather Guy, Hilary Gray, Janet Ashford, Gloria Preston, Beverly Guy, Dereck Caines.*

During the 1950s the use of the Village Hut as a venue for whist drives and village hops gradually declined. The structural condition of the building was also a cause for concern, and in May 1961, the trusteeship was transferred to the Parish Council on a 21-year lease. In August 1961 a public meeting was called to form a new Hut Management Committee and all village organisations were invited to attend. It was proposed that the committee should consist of one member from each village organisation, one Church member and one from the Parish Council. There would be no financial support from the Parish Council, and fund-raising activities would have to be organised to pay for the upkeep.

The condition of the Village Hut was discussed at a Parish Council meeting in July 1969. Extensive repairs were required, and there was only £180 in the current account; clarification was sought from the District Council as to what type of replacement building would be allowed on the site. A joint meeting with the Parish Council was held in November 1969, at which point repairs were required to the roof and floor of the building, as well as rewiring. The total funds available were only £250 and it was decided to obtain quotes for the repair work, and also to investigate the ownership of the land.

A further meeting took place in March 1970, when the legal position over the ownership of the land was explained. The land and building were owned by the vicar and churchwardens, and leased to the Parish Council on a 21-year lease, at an annual rent of one shilling. It was also stated that Council grants could not be obtained for repairs to Church huts. The Dorset Community Officer was present and stated that in his opinion it would be better to replace than repair, and that grants of up to £10 000 were available for this purpose. A further meeting took place in December 1970 when three options were discussed; repair, replacement or purchase of the primary school following its closure.

The Village Hut was destroyed by fire in January 1971; the cause of which event was believed to be faulty electrical wiring in the Sports Club's accommodation attached to the building, although this was never conclusively proven. A strong wind contributed towards the speed at which the fire spread, and poor water pressure also hampered the Fire Brigade's attempts to bring the blaze under control. The entire contents of the building were lost, with the only items salvaged being the banners of the former Friendly Society. Mr Robert Toone and Mr Ron Tite cleared the charred remains of the building from the site, and a three-year battle to build a new hall was initiated. A local paper of the time reported:

VILLAGE HALL GUTTED BY FIRE

Fire completely gutted the Stourton Caundle Village Hall, and the adjoining Young Men's Club, in an early morning blaze on Tuesday. Contents at the Hall, including a snooker table, were also destroyed. The Sturminster Newton Brigade went to the scene with two water tenders, and found the building ablaze from end to end. There was little we could do to save it, said Station Officer R. Clarke. The building was about fifty years old, and had a galvanised iron roof and sides, lined with plywood and timber. Mr Ronald Tite who lives near the hall discovered the fire. He was awakened by his young son, who was disturbed by a barking dog, and on looking out of a window he saw flames from the hall leaping into the sky. While his wife telephoned the Fire Service and Police, he ran to rouse neighbours, but there was nothing they could do to save the building, which within minutes was a mass of flames. Fire appliances from Sturminster Newton were quickly on the scene, remaining until 7a.m. Mrs Tite said that fortunately the wind was blowing in the right direction, otherwise the flames might have spread to a thatched roof on the other side of the hall.

THIS WAS A VILLAGE HALL

The Village Hall

A public meeting was held on 26 January 1971 to discuss the implications of the fire and elect a new Village Hall Committee. At a meeting on 23 February 1971 the Parish Council agreed to approach the vicar and churchwardens, requesting the legal transfer of the land on which the Village Hut had stood. Mr Frank Wharton, the Chairman of the Hut Management Committee, was asked to call an extraordinary meeting to wind up the affairs of the Committee and present a financial statement to the Parish Council. There was a vote of thanks to Mr Bob Toone and Mr Ron Tite for removing the debris from the site following the fire.

At the April meeting of the Parish Council it was agreed that the new Hall Committee should be properly constituted and answerable to the Parish Council. The committee would be responsible for the finances and management of the new Village Hall. The church commissioners had requested a valuation of the site, which had been completed and sent to Salisbury. A further public meeting was held in the September of 1972, attended by 50 parishioners. It was agreed to make a loan application to both the District and County Councils – this would not prejudice any future grant application. It was also approved that the Parish Council should levy the maximum rate for the parish, as this would be used as a basis for grant application.

The original cost had been estimated at £12 000, but by July 1972 the cost had risen to £16 000, and was still rising – to that date a total of £4448 had been raised. At a meeting of the Parish Council in December 1972, it was agreed to surrender the lease of the land to the vicar and churchwardens; the land could then be sold to the Parish Council at the agreed valuation. The land was valued at £500, and an agreement was made between Mr David Harris of Brunsells Farm and the churchwardens regarding the sale of a piece of land at Drove Road to provide an extension to the cemetery. This land was also valued at £500. Mr Harris then donated the money received from this sale to the Hall Committee to finance the purchase of the land on which the Village Hut had stood, from the Church.

The first AGM of the new Hall Committee was held in January 1973 when those present were informed that the total funds raised were £7738. Fund-raising activities included fortnightly bingo sessions, and a refreshment caravan sighted along the main holiday route to the West Country during summer weekends. The community spirit and enterprise shown by parishioners at this time, working together to achieve the common objective of a new Village Hall, can only be compared with the situation at the turn of the century, when the community's objective had been the preservation and restoration of the church.

With the legal problems over ownership of the land resolved, the funding in place and planning permission granted, construction work was at last able to start, the contract having been awarded to Gillham and Snook of Sturminster Newton. The building was completed and officially opened in May 1974. An annual dinner and dance was held each subsequent year, until escalating costs and dwindling support culminated in its cancellation. The One Hundred Club has provided a regular income, and enabled the facility to be maintained to a high standard. The current residents are indebted to the 1971 Committee for having the foresight to grasp the opportunity to provide the village with a first-class hall, designed to require only minimal maintenance, which will provide a meeting place for village organisations for generations to come.

The Young Men's Club

The Young Men's Club met three nights a week during the winter months. There were frequent clashes between the Club and the Hut Committee regarding the availability of the Hut, and over the planning of social events. Finally, in May 1929, the vicar, who was the Chairman of the Executive Committee, proposed that the Hut Committee should take over the assets and liabilities of the Young Men's Club and that the two organisations should combine to form one general committee. This proposal was implemented for a trial period of one year. At the first combined meeting in September 1929, Mr Mullett, who was representing the Club members, reported their dissatisfaction with the joint arrangement. At a meeting in October of the same year the Hut Executive Committee, which consisted of the vicar and churchwardens, resolved that the General Committee should be made up from five parishioners selected by them – together with two representatives from the Women's Institute, three from the Young Men's Club, and three from the church workers. A meeting was held in October 1930 to discuss a proposal to build an extension to the hut to provide separate accommodation for the Young Men's Club. Mr Cook the local builder generously offered to give both his own and his employees' services free of charge to erect the building, in accordance with the architect's plans. The extension was completed at a cost of £80 and opened on 18 November 1931. A full-size snooker table was purchased from Mr Kennard of Frith House for a sum of £24, dismantled and transported to the new clubroom by Pithers of Yeovil.

The dissension between the respective organisations still continued, and in the October of 1933 a joint committee was held to discuss a resolution that the Young Men's Club be allowed to manage their own affairs. The resolution was passed, with the annual rent for the use of the clubroom set at £10. The General Committee would pay for the rates, insurance and electricity. It was also agreed that the room and its contents were the property of the trustees, and the Club Committee also undertook to guarantee the good behaviour of the Club members. At a meeting held in February 1936 there was further disagreement between the two committees regarding the rent and share of the maintenance and running costs of the hut and clubroom. In February 1939 the Club was ordered to close by the Secretary of the Hut Committee but permission was granted to re-open on 1 October subject to the continued good conduct of the Club members. It was also agreed to discontinue the annual rent of £10 providing the Club agreed to pay for the heating, lighting and external maintenance of the clubrooms, and also a proportionate share of the rates and insurance.

In March 1948 discussions were held between the respective committees over the ownership of the premises, and it was agreed to seek legal advice from Mr Julius. The issue of ownership was never satisfactorily resolved; although the funds for the erection of the clubrooms had been raised by Club members, the land on which these rooms stood was owned by the trustees of the Village Hut, namely the vicar and churchwardens. An additional recreation room was added in the early 1950s, at a cost of £200, which meant that the Club could operate as a separate independent unit.

A programme of events was then organised by Sam Harris and Ted Foxwell to help clear the debt on the extension fund. This included a Guy Fawkes night celebration, which commenced with a children's fancy-dress competition, and a Guys parade, with more than 40 entries. There was a fireworks display in the orchard behind the hut, followed by an adult fancy-dress competition. The evening's entertainment concluded with dancing, to music provided by Dennis Holloway, with refreshments laid on by the Women's Institute.

Winners of the adult fancy-dress competition were: Most original: Mrs B. Lake (Black & White Minstrel); Mrs Parsons (Japanese Lady); Mr J. Clarke (Egyptian). Humorous: J. Gray/J.Guy/T.Lewis (Farmer with his Bull); Mr and Mrs Caines (Chiropodist and Patient); Mrs C. Dennett (Upside/Downside Man).

Over 60s Club

An Over 60s Club was formed in 1975. Following the appointment of Mrs Edith Brown as Chairman, the club grew to become one of the most active and best supported of village organisations, with a membership of current and former village residents. Coach outings are organised during the summer months, and a Christmas party was enjoyed at the December meeting. Fund-raising events include a Christmas bazaar and jumble sales. In 1999 Larry Skeats took over as Chairman and the club's name was changed to the Welcome Club in an attempt to attract some younger members.

Pensioners' Christmas parties held in the Village Hut in the 1960s.

The Sports Club

The Sports Club was formed in 1969, and took over the rooms and equipment of the defunct Young Men's Club, which included a full-size snooker table. The Hut was also hired on Club nights to provide additional accommodation for other activities such as table tennis. A football team was entered into division three of the Blackmore Vale Sunday League, and two teams entered into the Shaftesbury and District Table Tennis League. Mr Trevor Rowland was elected President of the Club, and he provided the football team with the use of a field behind Veales Cottage for home fixtures. Various fund-raising activities were organised, including a model aeroplane display at Rowden Mill Farm. Goal nets, goal posts and a second-hand set of kit were purchased in time for the start of the 1969/1970 season.

The first competitive match at home to Leigh resulted in a 2-2 draw. The following season the team achieved a famous cup victory against the Barbarians from Sherborne, by four goals to two after extra time. The team progressed from division three to division one of the league, and also appeared in two cup finals, losing one to Marnhull in a replay at Henstridge by four goals to two after extra time, the match being watched by several hundred spectators.

Following the 1971 Village Hut fire, the club relocated to temporary accommodation in the chapel. During this period the table tennis team won the third division of the league.

A gymkhana and exemption dog show was held on the spring bank holiday Monday of 1972. There were various other attractions and side shows, and on the Sunday evening prior to the event a service was held in the site marquee, conducted by the Reverend D.J. Hillier, with singing accompanied by Sherborne Town Band. The event was held again the following year, and the funds raised contributed towards the construction costs of the new clubroom.

In 1974, with members having played a significant part in fund-raising activities, the construction of the new Village Hall was finally completed, and the Club relocated to a new clubroom adjoining the building. The team disbanded in 1976 due to team members moving away from the village to pursue careers or further education. Dennis Shapland was the Secretary of the football team from its formation in 1969 until it disbanded at the end of the 1976 season. Throughout this period he worked tirelessly for the good of the team, in what was a very exciting period for all the team members, and for the club's officials and supporters. The Club continued with snooker, billiards and badminton, and a snooker team competes in the Sandford Orcas and District League. Mr Bill Perry is the oldest member, still playing snooker and billiards at the age of 91. There are annual cup competitions, with a presentation evening at the end of each season. Membership has declined significantly in recent years and the Club owes its continued existence to a small band of loyal members.

STOURTON CAUNDLE SPORTS CLUB

Annual Gymkhana
&
Exemption Dog Show

○○○○○○○○○○○○○○○○○○○○○○○

MONDAY, 29th MAY 1972
at
STOURTON CAUNDLE

(by kind permission of Mr. T. J. Rowland)

Gymkhana Events Commencing at 11 30 a.m.

Official Opening at 2 p.m. by
Mr. Ted Wilkins
Town Crier of Sherborne

Programme

11.30	Start of Gymkhana
	Ring One Group A 18 years and under
	Group B 13 years and under
12 noon	Refreshments and Licensed Bar
2 p.m.	Official Opening
	Start of Gymkhana Ring Two
	Group C 10 years and under
	Group D 7 years and under
2.10	Dog Show
	Numerous Stalls, Sideshows and Competitions for your entertainment
5 p.m.	Free Fall Parachute Display
5.45	The Draws will be made
6 p.m.	Selection of opponents for Junior Six-a-Side Football Tournament
6.15	Kick-off
7 p.m.	Selection of opponents for Tug-of-War
7.15	Tug-of-War (under A.A.A. rules)

All persons attending this event do so at their own risk. The Committee will not be responsible for any accident, loss or damage which may occur to any person, animal or property

Public Address Equipment by Mr. D. Holloway
Stalbridge

Licensed Bar by Henry and Muriel Harding
The Trooper Inn, Stourton Caundle

Club: Stourton Caundle
Colours: Amber Shirts-Black Shorts
Ground: Stourton Caundle
Secretary: Mr. D. Shapland
             2 Brimble Cottages
             Stourton Caundle
Telephone: Stalbridge 242
County: Dorset

The Club was formed in the spring of 1969 as the result of a public meeting called by Bernard Gray and Phil Knott, and named the Stourton Caundle Football Club. A team was entered in the third division of the Blackmore Vale Sunday League. With a very hard-working committee who organised various fund-raising events, the Club was able to take over the premises of the Young Men's Club, adjoining the Village Hut. With the aim of embracing former members of both the Young Men's Club, which had not been active since 1960, and the Youth Club which had closed following the departure of the Reverend Osborne in 1965, the Football Club was re-named the Stourton Caundle Sports Club. After having the premises re-wired, re-decorated and new heaters installed, it was opened in October 1970. By Christmas of that year membership had risen to over 30, with the Club opening twice weekly. In the early hours of a January morning in 1971 disaster struck when fire broke out in the premises, which were completely destroyed along with the adjoining Village Hut. This was a terrible blow, not only to the Sports Club, but also to every other village organisation.

STOURTON CAUNDLE SPORTS CLUB

President	Mr. T. J. Rowland
Chairman	Mr. R. I. Gillam
Vice Chairman	Mr. Peter Knott
Secretary	Mr. D. Shapland
Show Secretary	Mrs. T. J. Rowland
Treasurer	Mrs. Phillip Knott

Committee

D. Jenkins	S. Duffett	D. Cooke	D. Austin
M. Gray	B. Richardson	R. Toone	H. Paull

Left: *An extract from the 1972 Gymkhana programme.*

The Sports Club football team for the 1969–70 season.
Left to right, back: *Phil Knott, Dennis Reddicliffe, Peter Knott, Rex Cheeseman, Steve Shapland, Mike Edwards, Kim Howchin, John Howchin;*
front: *Bernard Gray, Des Austin, Malcom Gray, John Shapland, Tony Orchard, Brian Nettley.*

The Sports Club

*Dave Harris,
Chris Graham
and Bill Perry.*

Sports Club badminton players. left to
right: *Gerry Holdstock, Phil Knott, Sonia
Knott, Anna Lane, Margo Eavis, Lindsey
Saywell, Stewart Holdstock.*

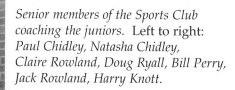

*Senior members of the Sports Club
coaching the juniors. Left to right:
Paul Chidley, Natasha Chidley,
Claire Rowland, Doug Ryall, Bill Perry,
Jack Rowland, Harry Knott.*

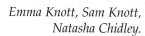

*Emma Knott, Sam Knott,
Natasha Chidley.*

Friendly Society

The Stourton Caundle Friendly Society was formed in 1836 with members contributing to provide some money in the event of sickness, unemployment and other misfortune. The scheme was financed by members' contributions, together with various fund-raising activities; any surplus funds were shared out between members on each Oak Apple Day, which was celebrated on 29 May each year to commemorate the restoration of the monarchy in 1660. The three banners belonging to the Society were paraded through the village, finishing at the Tithe Barn in Court Barton

Field, and any outstanding money raised from the previous year's subscriptions and fund-raising activities was then shared out between the members, followed by a fête, tea and dancing.

The Society's emblem mounted on a large banner was a skep bee-hive above clasped hands in the centre of a floral design, with bees and a scroll bearing the inscription; 'May we all strive together like bees of a hive and never sting each other.' The banner was rescued from the fire at the Village Hut and is now framed and mounted on the wall in the Village Hall.

The banner of the Stourton Caundle Friendly Society.

The 1922 Friendly Society procession.

The Slate Club

Another similar organisation was the Stourton Caundle Slate Club. The inaugural meeting was held at Newleaze Farmhouse on 1 November 1935. A committee and officers were elected by the 40 parishioners who attended the meeting, and trustees and auditors were also appointed. It was agreed that members could be accepted up to the age of 55 and that the committee would draft a set of rules for presentation to the next meeting. The proposed rules were presented to a meeting on 7 November, and passed with only some minor amendments. At a further meeting on 21 November, the Chairman read the final draft of the rules, which were approved by the meeting and duly signed by the Chairman and Secretary.

The Secretary was asked to obtain estimates for the printing of rulebooks, and also for the purchase of cash and accounts books. The Club organised fund-raising activities, such as whist drives and dances in the Village Hut. On 23 August a church parade was organised, starting from the Jubilee Oak at 6p.m., and headed by the standard bearers and the Boys Brigade Band from Sherborne, who had been engaged for the event at a fee of £3. The procession, including the Stalbridge Scouts Group, paraded through the village, around the triangle, and returned to the cricket ground at the rear of Veales Cottage for divine service at 7p.m. The banner of the former Friendly Society was repaired for the occasion by Mrs Gould of Newleaze farm, and Mr Fred Caddy made a wooden case in which to store it in the Young Men's clubroom.

Another procession was arranged for 11 August 1937, and the village's brass band formed for the Coronation celebrations in May of that year was at the head of the procession. The same route was followed as had been the previous year and after the procession the Reverend Fincher officiated at an open-air service, at which hymns were sung, accompanied by the band. The Annual General Meeting and share-out of money took place in December each year.

The Club continued throughout the war years with membership steady at well over 100 – with some members from Stalbridge Weston, Stalbridge and Thornhill. It finally disbanded in 1950, after the introduction of the National Health Service.

The Stourton Caundle Slate Club

BALANCE SHEET 1937.

RECEIPTS.	£	s.	d.		EXPENDITURE.	£	s.	d.
					Sick Pay—			
Entrance Fees	1	12	0		Sis. D. Furnell ...	3	16	8
Cards		8	9		„ W. Hedditch	3	6	6
109 Members Contributions	141	14	0		„ W. Stickland	2	0	0
1 „ lapsed		16	0		„ E. Orchard	1	11	8
Rules			6		„ F. Gummer	1	10	0
Fines ...		3	6		„ L. Lake		18	4
					„ A. Jeans ...		18	4
Honorary Subscriptions—					Bro. L. Jeans ...	5	7	6
Mr. Fernandes ...	1	0	0		„ H. Rose ...	4	15	0
Mr. Matthews ...		10	0		„ H. Brown ...	3	11	8
Entertainments	12	11	7		„ J. Harding	2	0	0
Church Parade	1	8	0		„ A. Walden	1	13	4
					„ C. Walden	1	0	
					„ L. Lake ...		18	
					„ S. Haime ...		18	4
					„ S. Scott ...		18	4
					„ F. Palmer ...		13	4
					Printing		17	0
Balance from 1936	5	7	4		Hire of Hut	1	10	0
					Cheques		6	6
					Secretary's Fee ...	5	10	0
					109 Members @ 21/-	114	9	0
					Retaining Fee ...	5	9	0
					Balance	1	13	2
	£165	11	8			£165	11	6

Audited and found Correct—A. M. HOLDWAY, E. M. GOULD.   December 4th, 1937.

H. J. HOLDWAY, Hon. Treasurer.   C. J. ORCHARD, Secretary.

STOURTON CAUNDLE SLATE CLUB
BALANCE SHEET 1949

Receipts	£	s	d		Expenditure / Sick Pay	£	s	d
65 Members @ 52/-.	169	0	0	Sisters. A.Watson	6	6	8
51 Members @ 26/-.'	66	6	0	D.Robson	4	0	0
4 Lapsed	3	2	0	W.Lane	3	16	8
1 Deceased		2	0	K.Light	4	10	0
				L.Cousins	2	18	4
				K.Brown	2	11	8
Entrance fees		9	0	V McKinnie	2	0	0
Cards		1	0	B.Lake	1	15	0
Death	6	6	0	Brothers T.Caddy	11	16	8
Fine		2	6	G.Trowbridge	5	13	4
				S.Everitt	5	10	0
				W.Hann	5	0	0
Hon Subscriptions				V.Caines	4	0	0
Miss Ludlow President	1	0	0	J.Riley	2	10	.0
				R.Tuffin	2	10	0
				J.Adams	3	6	8
				J.McKinnie	2	0	0
Whist Drive	8	12	6	H.Gawler	2	0	0
				M Knight	2	6	8
Balance Sheet from 1948	9	17	9	E.Bond	1	13	4
				L.Jeanes	2	0	0
				J.Gray	1	0	0
				H.Lane	1	0	0
				K.Knott	1	.0	0
				Death Levy	6	0	0
				Printing	2	0	5
				Cheques		10	0
				Secretary's fee	6	1	0
				Hire of Hut	1	0	0
				65 Members @ 35/-	113	15..	0
				51 Members @ 17/6	44	12	6
				Balance	8	13	0
	£264.	12.	9		£264	12	9

C.J. Orchard. (Secretary)
H.J. Holdway (Hon Treasurer)
Audited and found correct   A.E.Holdway.
                                   E.M. Gould.
12th December 1949.

Gardening Club

The Gardening Club was formed in 1974, and took over the running of the annual Flower Show under the stewardship of Miss Rosemary and Miss Helen Julius. The venue was switched to the new Village Hall, and the date of the Show changed from mid June to early September. The Club meets every month from October to March, normally with a guest speaker, and a Christmas party at the January meeting. The Gardening Club has followed the trend of all village organisations in recent years with falling membership and less exhibits at the annual Show and the Spring Show (which was held in the April of each year but which has now been discontinued). A local newspaper reported the event of the sixth annual Flower Show as shown below:

The 1980 Garden Club flower show.

SIXTH ANNUAL FLOWER SHOW

The sixth annual show of the Stourton Caundle Garden Club took place on Saturday. Fifty-one exhibitors (two less than last year) entered 365 exhibits (405 last year). The Judges' verdict was that the usual high standard had been maintained in all sections. As far as the children's section was concerned, there was an improvement, both in quality and quantity. The class for a handmade article produced a number of items, from sewing to woodwork. Hayden Williams' 'Matchstick House' earned him not only a first prize, but also the Hamilton cup for the best children's exhibit.

The Club's Chairman Miss R.M. Julius welcomed the Reverend D.J. Hillier, who presented the cups. Teas were organised by Mrs J. Foxwell and Mrs M. Burch, and

Mrs S. Burch and Mrs E. Pascow did a roaring trade on the plant and produce stall. Miss Jo Leslie-Jones was in charge of the "Buried Treasure" won by Anna Lane. The main competition winners were Mrs S. Simon, Mr R. Baillie, Miss H.M. Julius, Miss M. Page, Mrs E. Page, Lady Holland, Roderick Bealing, Mrs Mason and Mrs Wiles.

The trophy winners were as follows: Julius cup (Gentlemen's cup) – R.L. Baillie, who also won the Barnes cup for the best collection of vegetables, and the Salter cup for his exhibit of leeks in the any other vegetable class; Bond cup (Lady's cup) – Miss R.M. Julius; Baillie cup (Floral decoration) – Mrs S. Simon; Firth cup (Handicrafts) – R.J. Williams; Banksian Medal – P. Knott.

Youth Club

In May 1958 Mr S.J. Osborne was appointed as the vicar of the parish. He took a keen interest in the children of the village, and with the help of Mrs Peel from Higher Woodrow Farm formed a youth club, which met on a weekly basis in the Village Hut. Games such as table tennis were played, and records featuring the recording stars of the day were played on a Dansette record player. As well his pastoral duties

for the parish, Mr Osborne was also a mathematics teacher at Kings School, Sherborne, and during the summer months he arranged for the Youth Club to have the use of the school's swimming pool and tennis courts on Friday evenings. Free transport was provided, and after the evening's sporting activities were over, fish and chip suppers were purchased from Mr Quirks at Higher Westbury, Sherborne.

The Play Area

A proposal for a play area was first considered as part of the 1947 Post War Development Programme. At the inaugural meeting of the Parish Council in 1958, the provision of a play area was once again on the agenda, following problems with children encroaching on the designated allotment area, whilst playing in the street at Brimble. The proposal was dismissed as being too costly, and also an insurance risk. At a Parish Council meeting held in May 1973, a further complaint was received regarding boys playing football in the street, and causing a nuisance to a tenant. A suggestion was made that part of the allotments could be fenced off and used as a play area. At the following meeting in July of that year, it was stated that the allotment tenants were prepared to allow part of the site to be used as a play area. There was discussion as to whom would be responsible for fencing, and if any rent would be payable. The Clerk was instructed to write to the District Council in order to clarify the position. At the November meeting the location and size of the proposed area was discussed, as well as the need for ploughing, levelling and reseeding. At the next meeting of the Parish Council in May 1974, it was reported that the architect for the newly formed North Dorset District Council was considering proposals for development of the site, and it was decided to delay any decision on the plan.

At a meeting of the Parish Council in October 1976, the Chairman Mr Blades proposed that part of the allotment land at the bottom of Brimble could be used as a play area to celebrate the Silver Jubilee. This was generally felt to be a good idea, but at the following meeting the idea was shelved, with a lack of interest and complications with the site being the reasons given. In 1990 yet another attempt was made, a committee was formed and fund-raising events including a Christmas bingo were organised, but once again there was nobody with the enthusiasm and motivation to see the project through. Finally in 1994 Anna Lane formed a fund-raising committee of village parents, and started negotiations with the District Council for the provision of land. With the support of the Parish Council, a 21-year lease was arranged for redundant allotment land, and grant aid sought to help towards the provision of equipment. The Play Area Committee was reconstituted as the Play Area Management Committee, with delegated powers from the Parish Council for the management of the play area, and for the weekly safety inspections. The Parish Council was to take responsibility for the grass cutting and payment of the annual inspection fee. With the help of a group of volunteers the area was ploughed, levelled and reseeded, and a secure boundary fence was erected. The equipment was installed to the required safety standards. The play area was officially opened in June 1995. The maintenance and grass cutting was taken over by the Parish Council in 1999 following the disbandment of the Management Committee. This eventual triumph was reported in the local press:

Inset: *Dave Harris cuts the ribbon at the opening ceremony for the play area in July 1995.*

VILLAGERS WIN 38 YEAR PLAYING FIELD BATTLE

Young mothers from Stourton Caundle in North Dorset received the news last week, their parents were waiting to hear back in 1958. The village is at last going to have a designated play field, and after 36 years of waiting the mothers of 1994 are absolutely delighted. It was in 1958 that locals first mooted the idea of turning some spare land adjoining the allotments into a play area, and now thanks to the efforts of a new generation of parents the dream has at last come true.

Backed by the whole village *Mother of two Anna Lane said "The Parish Council and the whole village has backed us all the way. The North Dorset Housing Association, who intend to release part of the land for the building of low rent homes, have agreed to lease part of the land to the Parish Council for the play area. We can now fence it off and prepare the ground for the play equipment. We will need to raise £5000 to pay for the swings, slide climbing frames and other equipment. We already raised £630 from fund raising events."*

Friend and fellow helper Mrs Wendy Cooper, also a mother of two added "When we organised the petition for the play area, everyone in the village signed it, and thanks to the whole village the children at last have somewhere safe to play."

Village Outings

During the early years of the 20th century the annual day's outing to the seaside was the highlight of the year for village children. The parents and their children would assemble in the roadway at the Pound, which was situated opposite the school entrance. They would then climb excitedly aboard the horse-drawn farm wagons, and make themselves comfortable on bundles of clean straw for the journey to Stalbridge Station, to await the arrival of the steam train to take them on their way to the seaside. During the 1920s a fleet of charabancs were hired from a Mr Seager of Sherborne. The children would take a few coppers to school during the course of the year for the head-mistress to hold in safekeeping for them as spending money for the annual outing. The children would also help to raise money for their fares by taking part in a Christmas concert held in the Village Hut and the young men of the village would also contribute the collection from their Good Friday football match held in Meslams Field.

The route to Weymouth was down the Piddle Valley, and the same route and routine were followed each year. Packed lunches were taken, and the only treats the children could expect were an ice cream and a ride on a donkey. Afternoon teas were provided in the town, thanks to the generosity of the Fernandes family from Haddon Lodge, who travelled to Weymouth to meet the villagers at the restaurant and organise the seating arrangements. A child carrying a bucketful of sand and clutching a little wooden spade was a familiar site at the start of the journey home, with the mothers clutching a handful of seaweed to use as a barometer for the next twelve months. (The strip of seaweed (kelp) was hung on an outside wall near the back door. The nodules attached to the seaweed inflated during spells of dry weather, and deflated if wet weather was imminent.) There was singing and light-hearted banter on the way home, especially when passing the Cerne Giant (see *The Book of Cerne Abbas*). There was also a refreshment stop at a pub, this being the only occasion during the course of the year when the men and women present were able to escape from the harshness of every-day working life for just a few short hours.

The following recollection from one of those present sums up the importance of the annual outing to village children in those deprived pre-war years:

The children had been finding it difficult to concentrate on their lessons, because they were thinking of their forthcoming trip to Weymouth. The headmistress who had been reading a passage from a book, and aware of the pupils' lack of attention to what was being read, made a pretence of reading, quoting 'That the children of Stourton Caundle School seemingly have their heads full of nothing else than sea, sand and Weymouth rock.'

The outings restarted again after the war with a fleet of Bere Regis coaches for transporting families to the seaside destinations of either Weymouth or Swanage. By the late 1950s increasing car ownership and the introduction of a statutory paid week's holiday for farm workers sadly meant that there was no longer sufficient support for the annual outing.

The village outing. **Left to right:** *Harry Holdway, ? (behind), Ernest Cooke, Cecil Orchard (behind), Mrs Orchard, ?, Pam Parsons (with handbag), Mrs Bugg, Mary Orchard, Mrs A. Lane (behind), Mrs Priddle, Mrs Bugg (behind), Mrs A. Bealing, Mrs Osmond (behind), Billy Dare, Mrs R. Knott (behind), Mrs Oliver, Mrs Dare, Mrs M. Stainer, Jean Parsons (in white ankle socks), ?, Mrs Gwinnurth, Sandra Gwinnurth (white bow in hair), Mrs Dennett, Mrs Bond (behind), Lena Bond, ?.*

Village Outings, 1920s

Village Outings, 1920s

Left to right, back: *Mrs Dennett, Mrs Galpin, Kate Ashford, Mrs Oliver, visitor from London, Mrs Winter, Mr Sibley (bus driver), ?, Eva Furnell, Mrs M. Lane (behind), Syd Lane (behind wearing cap), Mrs Lane, Mrs A. Caddy;* Front: *children, visitors, Mrs Gummer, Mrs Bugg, Ruby Bugg.*

A late 1920s village outing about to depart for Weymouth.

The author's mother is wearing the white bonnet, and is standing immediately behind the four adult front-seat passengers.

Pre-war Cricket

During the summer evenings of 1933 boys and men of all ages met at Court Barton field to play cricket. The only equipment available was a bat, which had been hewn from a plank of wood, and a badly battered cricket ball. Several collections took place amongst the players and spectators, which provided sufficient funds for the purchase of a bat and cricket ball.

A number of meetings were held at the Young Men's Club during the winter of 1934, and the members decided to form a cricket team. An immediate start was made to raise funds for the purchase of equipment, and a variety of events were organised. A fixture list was drawn up, to include evening and Saturday afternoon matches, against teams from neighbouring villages. Fixture cards were printed, and sold for a shilling each, and permission was obtained for the use of a field at the rear of Veales Cottage. A small area was roped off for the preparation of a wicket, of a suitable condition for the start of the season. The team members constructed a pavilion, supervised by Mr Fred Caddy. The summer of 1934 proved to be a successful one for the club, and it was decided to enter a knockout competition for the 1935 season.

The first round match was an away fixture at Shillingstone and resulted in a heavy defeat. However the 1935 and 1936 seasons were successful for the club, with a substantial number of matches played all over North Dorset resulting in victories for the village team. Towards the end of the 1936, there was a substantial reduction in the numbers of players available for selection for away matches. The Club disbanded shortly after the start of the 1937 season, following the loss of a number of the better players, leaving insufficient numbers to field a competitive team.

Pre-war Football

During the 1930s, football was played in Meslams Field during the light summer evenings. Most of the village lads worked on the local farms, and were unable to play in competitive matches on Saturday afternoons. A regular Good Friday match was played in Meslams field between the married and single men of the village. Evening friendly matches were also played against neighbouring villages during the light summer evenings. Before the match, small boys were given the job of keeping a herd of grazing cattle away from the playing area, while the men used shovels to clear the numerous cow pats. The four uprights for the goal posts had been cut from a local coppice, and two ash poles were used as crossbars. There were no goal nets until the mid 1930s.

Heated arguments often occurred when the ball went out of play, as the linesman did not have the benefit of white lines. The corner and halfway marker posts were adorned with rag to help them make a decision. They were often on the receiving end of abuse from spectators who disagreed with the decisions they had made. It was not unusual for a linesman to throw down his flag in disgust, leaving the match to continue without a linesman as nobody else was prepared to take on the thankless task. The team became known locally as the League of Nations, as it was rare to see more than two team members wearing the kit of the same colour and design. There was intense rivalry between the local teams, each side believing it was a matter of honour to win for their respective village.

An away match at Stalbridge Weston took place on a humid summer's evening in a field next to the New Inn. The heat was stifling, and soon the players were to feel its effect on their breathing, movement and stamina. A spectator provided a large bucket of water, and the players left the pitch at will, in order to replenish their thirst. The referee did the same leaving the match to continue without him. An away match at Lydlinch was played in the pouring rain in a field directly opposite the turning to Bagber. The referee fell headfirst into a pool of muddy water, rendering his whistle useless, for most of the second half. He controlled the remainder of the match by shouting his decisions at the top of his voice, and waving his arms. After the match, the players stopped at the Three Boars Heads until closing time, before staggering home. During the autumn of 1935, an application was made to join a local league, and a benefactor donated five pounds towards the purchase of a second hand goal posts and goal nets. The proceeds from several dances held in the hut, met the cost of a purchase of a set of shirts, with a pattern of dark blue and white squares. The application for the 1935/36 season was turned down on the grounds that the forms had been submitted too late. Enthusiasm waned following this setback, and although friendly matches continued to the outbreak of the Second World War, no further attempt was made to join a league.

Women's Institute

The Women's Institute was formed in 1926, and met on a monthly basis at the Village Hut. At a special meeting held on 18 December 1942, called by the Secretary of the County Federation, new officers were elected by the members in a ballot, which followed the rules and procedures of the County Federation. Mrs Fernandes was re-elected President in recognition of her past work for the Institute, although it was felt unlikely that she would be able to attend future meetings due to failing health. Mrs Holdway and Mrs Westhall were elected Vice Presidents, and Mrs Stainer, the retiring Treasurer, was thanked for her 14 years of service. Following this meeting two books were kept, one to record the minutes of the committee meetings, and the second to record the activities of the monthly meetings.

On 7 January 1947, the Institute celebrated its 21st birthday with a party at which 100 members and friends were present. The format of the monthly meetings included a guest speaker, followed by refreshments and a social half-hour, which included such activities as games, riddles, dancing to the accompaniment of a piano, and community singing.

Whist Drives were organised on a regular basis to raise funds for the children's Christmas party and the annual village outing, with members contributing 6d. each towards the prizes. A New Year's party was held in the early January of each year, the first part consisting of games and competitions. After the refreshments the remainder of the evening was spent dancing to the accompaniment of the band, the members of which were Harry Holdway, Ambrose Stainer, Frank Palmer and George Harris.

The Institute disbanded in 1986 due to insufficient membership and the minute books and other records are deposited in the county archives at Dorchester. These provide a revealing insight into the decline in the social activity and community spirit in the parish which resulted in the demise of a once vibrant and thriving village organisation.

Women's Institute members on Oak Apple Day, May 29 1937. Picture taken at Whitemead Jubilee oak, prior to the Friendly Society Procession through the village. Left to right, back: Rose Bugg, Dot Lightgo, Maltilda Bugg, Mrs Gummer, Kate Brown, Mary Stainer, Mabel Fernandes, Enid Fernandes, Ruby Winter, Gertrude Star, Edith Orchard; front: Annie Bealing, Ruby Bealing, Mrs Read, Elsie Galpin, Florence Dennett, Annie Caddy, Marjorie Lane, Ada Lane.

The WI County Rally held at Milton Abbey, 1942.
Left to right: Mrs Briddle, Mrs Bealing, Mrs Knott.
The banner is now on display in the Village Hall.

Stourton Caundle
Women's Institute

PROGRAMME 1981

President   Mrs E. PAGE
Wagtails, Stourton Caundle
Tel: Stalbridge 62082

Vice - President   Mrs J. FIRTH

Secretary   Mrs A. HARRIS

Assistant Sec.   Mrs A. MONK

Group Sec.   Mrs W. HAMILTON

Treasurer   Mrs I. FOXWELL

Meetings held every 3rd Wednesday
in each month at 7.30 p m

Women's Institute evening outing to Bulbarrow in 1952. Left to right, back (standing): Mrs Mullett, Mrs
Bugg, ?, Mrs A. Bealing, Mrs Stainer, Mrs Bugg, Mrs Parsons, Syd Lane, Mrs Lane,
Mrs Holdway, Mrs Lake, Mrs Caddy, Mrs Baverstock, Mrs Brooks, Kathleen Brooks;
front (kneeling): Mrs Orchard and Mary, ?, Mrs Guy, Mrs R. Bealing and Eric,
Mrs Ashford with ?, Mrs Galpin.

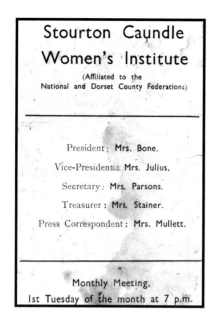

Stourton Caundle Women's Institute

(Affiliated to the National and Dorset County Federations)

President: Mrs. Bone.

Vice-President: Mrs. Julius.

Secretary: Mrs. Parsons.

Treasurer: Mrs. Stainer.

Press Correspondent: Mrs. Mullett.

Monthly Meeting,
1st Tuesday of the month at 7 p.m.

WI Christmas party, 1961. Left to right, back: Mr F. Baverstock, Mr M. Lane, ?, ?, Mrs J. Chaffey, Mrs A. Bealing, Mrs Bugg, ?, Mrs Bradbury, ?, Mrs M. Lane; middle: ?, Mrs Phillips, ?, ?, ?, ?, Mrs Perry, ?, ?, ?, Mrs Paine; front: Mrs Brown, Mrs Swaffield, Revd Osborne, ?, Mrs Screen, Mrs Else, Mrs R. Bealing, Mrs Baverstock.

Village Open Weekends

Three village open weekends have been held, the first of which was organised by the Parochial Church Council in July 1986 to raise funds for the church. A dozen gardens were open to visitors, and there was a floral display in the church, with cream teas being served in the garden of the Old Vicarage. The Village Hall was the setting for a display of local arts and crafts with over 25 displays and disciplines being exhibited, together with an exhibition of old photographs collected by Nigel Orchard. The second weekend was organised by a village committee, and took place in June 1994 under the chairmanship of Col Craw. The main purpose of this event was to raise money for the Church Repair Fund – a total of £26 000 was required for repairs to the roof and structural repairs to the gardens at Manor Farm. There were various other attractions including demonstrations of hurdle making and sheep shearing at this event.

Following the success of this weekend the 1995 event was expanded to include other attractions such as a farrier shoeing horses, and a thatching demonstration. An exhibition of old photographs was staged in the Village Hall, and a marquee was erected at the rear of the Trooper Inn which was used to accommodate craft stalls. On the Friday evening a country and western band performed in the marquee, and on the Saturday evening a school reunion took place; nearly all the post war pupils who had attended the village primary school had been contacted. There was a barbecue and hog roast, and fifties and sixties

music helped former pupils revive memories of their schooldays. During the daytime on both Saturday and Sunday the main street was closed to through traffic, and visitors were directed around Wheel to a car park in Ropers Field. An auction of rural bygones and collectables took place on the Saturday morning, and the total proceeds from the two days of events were divided equally between St Peter's, the Village Hall and the children's play area.

Stourton Caundle
Village Open
Sat. June 24th.
and
Sun. June 25th.
1995

Programme of Events. 2op

Gardens Open - also Lakes

Tickets available opposite the Trooper Inn

Attractions

See Craftsmen at Work

Wood turning   Hurdle making

Thatching   Farrier - Shoeing

Sheep Shearing (Sat and Sun 2.30 and 4.30 p.m.)

Vintage

Motorbikes - Tractors - Engines - Cars

Plant Stalls • Shire Horse Rides • Herb Stall

Ferret Racing • Fairground Organ • Cake Stall

Skittle Alley Museum   •   Try a "Horn of Cider"

Dog Show   •   Tombola   • Hand Bell Ringing

For the Children

Punch and Judy - 3.30 and 4.30 pm. Sat only

Magic - 4.00 pm Sat only.

Face Painting - Sat only.

(all of the above in Brunsell Farm Barn)

Childrens Fun Area

Sponge Throwing • Splat - the - Rat • Bouncy Castle

Open Weekends

CHAPTER 8

THE WAR YEARS

The Home Guard

Following the fall of Dunkirk, and with the imminent threat of invasion, the Secretary of State for War Sir Anthony Eden announced in a wireless broadcast on 14 May 1940 the proposed formation of a Citizens Army, to be known as the Local Defence Volunteers. He asked for men between the ages of 17 and 65 who were willing to join to report to their local Police Station. Men of all ages and backgrounds who were not eligible for call-up volunteered and in the next few weeks officers were appointed, and local platoons formed. In July 1940 Winston Churchill announced a change of name, to the more positive sounding Home Guard. In the early days there was no equipment or uniforms, other than armbands displaying the letters LDV. Later that year denim battle dress was provided, and was worn over everyday clothing. Eventually proper Army battle dress was provided, with black boots, leather gaiters, belted greatcoats, haversacks, gas masks and helmets.

The Home Guard. Left to right, back: *Charlie Dennett, Dick Winter, Frank Hollex, Dennis Jeanes, Eddy Bond, Frank Palmer, Sonny Bealing, George Lane;* middle: *Albert Bealing, Roy Brown, George Brown, Leslie Woods, Joe Walden, Len Lake, Jack Watson, Alex Smith;* front: *Billy Bugg, Charlie Lake, Cecil Orchard, the Sergeant, George Furnell, Bob Green, Jack Pye, Jim Gray.*

At the start volunteers were asked to provide whatever weapons they had of their own, and an assortment of old rifles, farmers' shotguns, antiquated swords and knives were used, and as a last resort pickaxes and pitchforks. Lee Enfield rifles and Lewis guns later replaced these weapons. The volunteers from Stourton Caundle formed part of the Lydlinch Platoon, and during the Autumn of 1939 Army manoeuvres took place at Lydlinch Common. Air-raid shelters were also constructed in the gardens of local houses and cottages. These were often little more than a hole in the ground, covered by sheets of corrugated iron. On 16 May 1940, a football match took place in Meslams Field between a local team and a team of soldiers from the Scottish Highland Regiment based at Venn House, Milborne Port. They came by lorry, changed into their blue and white strip at the Trooper Inn, and marched to the field in military procession. After the match dancing took place outside the Trooper Inn, with the soldiers wearing full Scottish dress, and dancing to the accompaniment of drums and bagpipes. The return match was cancelled at short notice, the regiment having formed part of the expeditionary force to France, where sadly a number of them perished on the beaches at Dunkirk.

In 1940 at the height of the invasion scare all road directional signs were removed, lectures were held in the village hut for the LDV members, and overnight patrols were carried out on the high ground at the top of Holt Lane. There were two four-hour shifts to look out for German parachutists, these were desperate times, and the LDV had no weapons or uniforms. On the night of 7 September 1940, the code word Cromwell was issued by military command, to warn of an imminent invasion. The members of the LDV were aroused from their beds and told to report to the front of the Trooper Inn for emergency overnight standby, no further orders were issued, and the volunteers spent the night talking and trying to keep warm.

Following the invasion scare many changes were made, three rifles and a few rounds of ammunition were issued for use on guard duty, and regular patrols were mounted at the top of Cat Lane near Brunsells Knapp. It was decided to use the redundant cricket pavilion as a guardroom, and it was relocated to a field at Brunsells Knapp. A derelict cottage at Goldsneys was taken over as the HQ rifle practice took place in an orchard at the rear of Barrow Hill Farm, and a small building was constructed at the bottom of the orchard which was used for storing explosives.

The unit had become part of the Lydlinch Platoon of the Home Guard, more stringent military discipline was introduced, and service in the unit became compulsory for all adult males in the parish. Military training included the use of hand grenades, and .303 calibre rifles. Night-training exercises took place at Stock Gaylard and Lydlinch Common. The Home Guard was disbanded on 31 December 1944, and a demobilisation parade through the village was followed by a thanksgiving service held in St Peter's Church. The money raised for the unit's benevolent fund was used to stage a party for the village children.

The demobilisation parade in 1944, passing the ruins of the former terrace of four thatched cottages and the Reading Room, which were located opposite the Pound.

Air Raid Precautions

Village men of all age groups had volunteered to learn the correct way of dealing with incendiary devices dropped from enemy aircraft, and they were known as fire-watchers. Mr Harry Holdway who lived at Barrow Hill Farm had been appointed Air Warden. At the height of the German bombing campaign in 1940 and 1941, a unit consisting of three men would be on duty throughout the night. When a red alert was received by telephone from military command, the wardens would sound the alert by blowing short blasts on their whistles as they toured the village to warn the sleeping residents. After the all clear had been given, the exercise would be repeated, but this time giving long blasts on the whistles. During this period wave after wave of German bombers could be heard passing overhead, on their way to the industrial cities and ports in the Midlands and the North.

The only bombs dropped locally were a single bomb in a field at Rowden Mill Lane, and a stick of five bombs in a field at Brunsells Knapp. A line of bombs was also dropped at Brick Hill, the last one dropping down a disused well near the cottages, causing some minor structural damage – although there were no casualties.

A searchlight battery operated by a small unit of regular soldiers was located at Rowden Mill Lane, in Brookhill Field, and when it was in operation, fingers of light could be seen criss crossing the night skies above the village.

In addition to the fire-watchers there was also an auxiliary fire crew. The fire engine which they used was located in a garage at Drove Road, opposite the Old Vicarage and members of the crew included Sam Harris and Jack Osmond.

The Evacuees

Some 19 evacuees, aged from five to nine years old, arrived by train at Stalbridge Station during early September, 1939. They were collected by volunteers and transported to the Village Hut where they were greeted by the billeting officer Miss Starr, and provided with tea. Each child was then issued with a blanket, collected by their temporary guardians, and taken to their new homes. By March 1940, all but one boy of the first group to arrive in the village had returned to London. Henry Finch remained at the village primary school until 1942, and then transferred to Stalbridge High School. During the remainder of the war period a number of other evacuee children spent time billeted in the village and attended the primary school.

Those who gave their lives

1914 – 1918

Hubert Henry Bugg
Thomas James Caddy
Albert Edward Carter
Alfred Joseph Hann
Lionel Charles Jeanes
Henry Osmond

1939 – 1945

S. J. Haime
D. G. Furnell

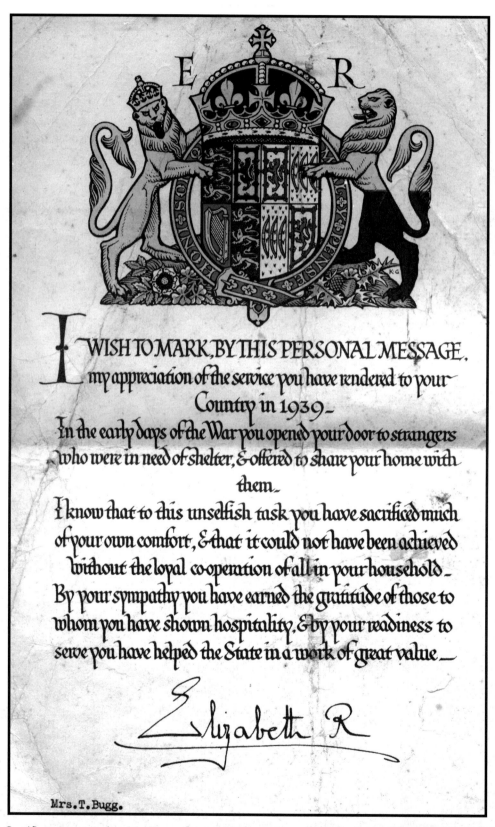

Certificate presented to Mrs Bugg for providing accommodation and care for evacuee children.

CHAPTER 9
SPECIAL EVENTS

A procession arranged to celebrate the 1911 Coronation of King George V started from Jubilee Oak and was headed by a brass band. The flags of the village societies were on parade.

The 1935 procession for the Silver Jubilee celebrations for King George V.

The 1937 Coronation

The celebrations for the 1937 Coronation of King George VI started with a parade from Jubilee Oak, which passed down through the village, around the triangle, and back up the High Street, finishing in the orchard adjoining the cemetery. Walter Hays and Harry Holdway are at the head of the procession.

Mrs Winter, Mrs Gould, Mrs Stainer and Mrs Mullett (with banner)
at the head of the Women's Institute contingent.

The 1937 Coronation

*After the procession games and sports competitions took place in the orchard at the rear of the Village Hut,
and the village band played a selection of tunes from its small repertoire during the afternoon's events.*

The 1937 Coronation

A village brass band was formed to celebrate the 1937 Coronation of King George V. Marching rehearsals took place in Drove Road, and the band was at the head of the procession on Coronation day on 12 May.

Nos 1 and 2 Veales Cottages decorated for the Jubilee celebrations.

Mr. & Mrs. G. W. L. Fernandes will be very pleased if

Mr. & Mrs. H. Bealing

will come to Supper with them in Stourton Caundle Church Hut on Wednesday, 12th May, at 7 p.m.

In the evening a supper was provided by Mr and Mrs Fernandes of Haddon Lodge. All parishioners were invited to attend and the meal was followed by a dance to music played by the village band, which completed the day's celebrations.

1953 Coronation

A village committee was elected at a public meeting to arrange the celebrations for the Coronation of Queen Elizabeth II. Rosemary and Helen Julius were elected joint secretaries. The day's celebrations started with a children's fancy-dress competition held outside the Trooper Inn. After the judging the children took their places in the procession through the village starting from the Jubilee Oak and headed by Mr Ambrose Stainer playing his trumpet, and Mrs Betty Toone with her piano accordion. The children were presented with Coronation mugs at an afternoon tea party. Bunting and flags were on display throughout the village, looking rather bedraggled due to heavy overnight rain. The events in Westminster Abbey were broadcast live on television, eagerly watched in a crowded lounge bar at the Trooper Inn on one of only three television sets installed in the village at that time.

To complete the day's celebrations an evening dance was held in the Village Hut. The remaining funds were used to purchase six commemorative trees, which were planted by Frank Palmer and Mick Ashford. Three of these, a laburnum opposite the church, a may tree at the Pound and a flowering cherry on the verge opposite Trooper Cottage, have survived.

The start of the 1953 Coronation procession.

Ambrose Stainer playing his trumpet leads the 1953 Coronation procession.

The 1953 Coronation

Mary Orchard and Philip Knott, participants in the fancy-dress competition.

Sherbourne Town Band parading through the village before providing the music for the Sunday evening marquee service prior to the Gymkhana and Dog Show held on the Whitsun Bank Holiday Monday, 1973.

1977 Silver Jubilee

A public meeting was called by the Village Hall Committee following a request to them by the Parish Council to organise the Silver Jubilee celebrations for Queen Elizabeth II. The Chairman, Mr David Harris, asked the meeting to elect an independent Chairman, and for each village organisation to appoint a representative to serve on the committee. Mr David Perris was elected Chairman, and Miss Helen Julius Secretary. A fête held in the paddock at the rear of Wagtails, the residence of Mr and Mrs Page during the summer of 1976, helped to raise funds for the Jubilee celebrations and project. The Silver Jubilee parish project was to restore the church clock, converting it to electric drive and fitting hands to the clock face. The event was recorded by Mr Monk on a 16mm cine camera; the film survives and edited highlights are in the video film recording the 20th-century history of the parish.

The day's programme for the celebration of the Silver Jubilee included a fancy-dress competition, a parade headed by a band, rides in a pony and cart and a comic football match, which took place in Ropers Field. An evening party in the Village Hall completed the day's events.

The children's fancy dress competition at the 1977 Silver Jubilee celebrations

Silver Jubilee

Top: *Dave Perris, Chairman of the Jubilee Committee.*
Above: *Cyril Knott with his pony and trap.*

Roderick and Philip Bealing.

*Stourton Caundle children attending All Saints Primary School at
Bishops Caundle, planting a tree to commemorate the Silver Jubilee.*

Children's street party to celebrate to wedding the Prince Charles and Princess Diana.

The planting of an oak sapling in 1987 to replace the Jubilee oak planted to commemorate the Diamond Jubilee of Queen Victoria. Three attempts have been made to plant a fruitful oak; the third of which, in the autumn of 1999, will hopefully prove successful.

The football teams for the V.E. Day match.

Left to right, back: *Roy Moorse, Dick Dowden, Steve Neal, Larry Skeats, Dave Richardson, Dave Gray, Phil Knott;* front: *Sue Knott, Shane Pullen, Pat Pike, Deborah Stafford.*

Left to right, back: *Larry Yandle, Albin Harris, Peter Knott, Albin Guy, Dave Harris, Frank Bastable, Chris Vining;* front: *Katie Guy, ?, Micheala Ralph, Priscilla Harris.*

VE Anniversary Celebrations

The Victory in Europe celebrations in the May of 1995 were centred on the Trooper Inn combined with a comic football match, which took place in Ropers Field. Following a photo call at the front of The Trooper, the two teams paraded through the pub car park, and down to Ropers Field. The two captains – Dave Harris, resplendent in his kilt and wearing a sporran, and Larry Skeats – were bearing flags at the head of their respective teams, and union flags and bunting were also draped at the front of the Trooper. The match referee Mr Dennis Fairclough from Bishops Caundle, wearing a dinner jacket and top hat, had difficulty in keeping control of a competitive match. The highlight of the first half was a fine save by the red-team goalkeeper Dave Harris, diving acrobatically across the goal mouth to save a goal bound shot at the foot of his left-hand post. There were a number of incidents both on and off the ball, finally culminating in some verbal abuse, and physical contact between the two captains. This resulted in Dave Harris ending up spread-eagled on the ground, with his kilt raised above his knees, only narrowly failing to reveal whether or not he was wearing anything underneath. The referee had no option but to show them both a red card, and after vehemently protesting their own innocence, and blaming each other for causing the affray, they finally left the field of play.

During the second half a number of substitutions were made, with the introduction of younger players increasing the tempo of the game. The stretcher party was also required for Cilla Harris who sustained a leg injury, and first-aid man Syd Duffett was on hand to provide assistance. The full-time score was one goal each, and a penalty shoot-out was required to separate the teams.

After the match a barbecue was held in the pub car park on a warm sunny spring evening. Wartime songs were relayed over a loudspeaker system to recreate a forties atmosphere, and the evening finished with a fifties and sixties disco in the skittle alley to set the seal on a very successful evening.

Tree planting for the VE Day celebrations. Left to right: *Paul Knott, Adam Knott, Mathew Williams, Rebecca Owen, Naomi Holdstock (with spade), Helen Dike, Stuart Holdstock, Harry Dike.*

STRAWBERRY FAYRE

STOURTON CAUNDLE 18 JUNE 2000

PROGRAMME 50P

Programme of Activities

12.00 Noon	Lunchtime BBQ	Trooper Inn

2.00 p.m.	Opening Ceremony
	Phil Street
	Dorset Champion Town Crier

2.30 p.m.	Children's Fancy Dress Competition
	Under 8 years and Over 8 years
2.30 p.m.	Family Dog Show
	Many Classes - All Dogs Welcome
3.00 p.m	Judging of Scarecrow Competition
3.00 p.m.	Strawberry Cream Teas
	at Manor Farm
3.00 p.m.	Tennis Final Manor Farm
	The Sports Club Room in the Village Hall will be open throughout the afternoon
3.30 p.m.	Children's Sports including Splat the Rat
3.30 p.m.	Demonstration of Fly-Casting

5.00 p.m.	Bell-Ringing at St Peter's Church
5.30 p.m.	Evening Service with Father Nigel Orchard followed by Cheese and Wine

Stourton Caundle Strawberry Fayre

Car Treasure Hunt
Saturday Evening
starting from the Village Hall
between 5.00 p.m. and 6.00 p.m.
followed by a Barbecue
at the Trooper Inn

The Church of St Peter,
founded in the 13 Century,
will be open throughout
Sunday afternoon.
Come and see
the floral decorations

Don't forget to buy your ticket
for the
Stourton Caundle Village Raffle
First Prize £100

The proceeds from the Strawberry Fayre will be distributed amongst the village community groups which have worked hard to organise the events of the day - the Parish Church, the Parish Council, the Garden Club, the Welcome Club, the Sports Club and the Village Hall Committee.

Millennium Strawberry Fayre

During the autumn of 1999 a village committee was formed to organise a Strawberry Fayre. The committee met on a regular basis during the winter and spring months to plan the event, which took place the following June to celebrate the start of the new millennium. Prior to the event Terry Taylor and Andrew Oliver organised a general-knowledge quiz, with 18 teams participating, and on the Saturday evening Phil Knott organised a car treasure hunt which finished with a barbecue, and live music provided by Ben Bennett's band at the rear of the Trooper Inn. On the Sunday the road was closed to through traffic, which was diverted around Wheel. The visitors to the fayre were directed along Drove Road, to a car park at the rear of the Village Hall. The various stalls and side-shows were set up either side of the street, from the bottom of Golden Hill to the grassed area at the Pound.

Each village organisation had their own stall, and the income from the remaining stalls was put into a communal pot, which was divided equally between the six village organisations after the event. The opening ceremony was carried out by the Town Crier from Lyme Regis. Attractions included an exhibition of photographs and memorabilia staged by Phil Knott in the Village Hall. The Parish Meeting and Parish Council minute books dating from 1896 were also on display, together with the school admission records from 1913. The first pupil listed in the records, Miss Ada Lane, was still resident in the village, and attended the event. The minute books and admission records were subsequently placed in the County Records Office at Dorchester.

The first part of the video film recording the 20th-century history of the village was also on view, and attracted much interest. Other features included a children's fancy-dress, and a best scarecrow competition, which was judged by Miss Rosemary Julius. There were demonstrations of sheep shearing by Larry Skeats, and hurdle making by 86-year-old Mr Harris from Farnham. A cart pulled by two Shire horses provided rides around the village, and there were children's sports in Ropers Field. Mr Malcom Gray acted as judge for the dog show. There was a floral display in St Peters Church, and strawberry and cream teas were served at Manor Farm. The event finished with a service of thanksgiving conducted by Father Nigel Orchard, followed by a cheese and wine party. The whole of the day was bathed in glorious sunshine, with not a single cloud in the sky, to set the seal on what proved to be one of the most successful and best supported community events in recent years.

*Randy Hiscock with his pair of Suffolk Punch horses provided rides,
which proved popular with both children and adults.*

Strawberry Fayre

Dave Harris, Ralph Mowatt and Cindy Dowden.

Sue Knott and Jane Yandle on the Gardening Club plant stall.

Olive Rowland and Priscilla Harris (back to camera) on the tombola stall in aid of the Village Hall.

STOURTON CAUNDLE STRAWBERRY FAYRE
SUNDAY, 18 JUNE 2000

It is now less than a month to the date of the Strawberry Fayre and you will remember from our previous letter that we would like as many people as possible in the village to join in and help make this a truly memorable occasion. With this in mind, there will be

A Public Meeting on Tuesday, 30 May
in the Skittle Alley of the Trooper Inn
at 19.30

We hope that many village residents will come along.

The Strawberry Fayre will be opened at 14.00
by Phil Street, Dorset Champion Town Crier.

Programmes will be available nearer the day but some activities, such as the Tennis Tournament, are already under way. Watch the village notice boards for progress.
For some events advance information is important:
  Fancy Dress Competition for children ('Under 8s' and 'Over 8s')
  Scarecrow Competition
  Car Treasure Hunt on Saturday 17 June starting from the Village Hall Car Park between 17.00 and 18.00 and followed by BBQ on return.
  Family Dog Show

A full programme of other attractive events and activities will take place on Strawberry Fayre Day.
A number of produce stalls will be run by some of the village organisations and contributions will be very welcome. The Garden Club would like to receive plants (named if possible), vegetables, fruit, jams, pickles and books on gardening.

The Draw for the **Village Raffle** (First Prize £100) will be made at the end of the day. Donations for Prizes will be much appreciated and should be made to David Harris, Brunsell Farm, tel 364034, by Thursday 15 June.

The Fayre will close with a Service in St Peter's Church at 17.30. The Service will be taken by Father Nigel Orchard. After the Service everyone is invited to Cheese and Wine in the Church.

Contacts: Larry Skeats (362405), Dick Dowden (363510) Jane Colville (362287)

Come along to the meeting on Tuesday, 30 May.

STOURTON CAUNDLE STRAWBERRY FAYRE 18/06/2000

COMMUNITY FUND INCOME			EXPENSES		
Pub Quiz	100	-	WDDC draw licence	35	-
Donation Tony Bond to be	300	-	Blackmore vale ad	4	35
retained as bank deposit			Blackmore vale ad	108	51
Teas	310	-	Paid to Jane Colville for baps	182	20
Strawberries sold at gate	84	-	Dikes, wine, cheese, squash &		
Strawberries sold afterwards	21	20	heavy horse hire (£60)		
BBQ	170	20	Paid to Sue Simon cream,	133	25
Donation Jane Colville for Heavy	40	-	sausages, tea, strawberries, etc		
Horse hire			Band	150	-
Horse rides	60	-	Dorset graphic art for printing	55	65
Donation to raffle Brian Page	50	-	draw tickets		
Returned raffle prize by Ray Foot	100	-	Ralph Mowat printing costs	39	89
Raffle	650	-	Marquee hire 50%	25	-
Ice cream	13	-	Transport	15	-
Swings	8	-	Shearing	15	-
Rent from stalls	25	-	Town Crier	30	-
Treasure hunt and barbecue	61	80	Prize cards and badges	5	-
Auction of wheelbarrow	20	-			
Circus and face painting	10	-	**TOTAL EXPENSES**	**798**	**85**
Sale of sheep fleeces	5	-			
Trooper Inn program sale	25	-			
Program sale on day	19	-	**OTHER INCOME**		
TOTAL	**2,072**	**20**	Garden Club	152	-
- EXPENSES	**798**	**85**	Church Stalls cake £127.43,	192	83
PROFIT	**1,273**	**35**	books £58.40, Dip £7.00		
			Welcome Club	206	-
Left in bank as deposit	300	03	Church Flowers	62	-
Remaining	973	32	(£30 donated to Church)		
Divided equally between Parish			Village History Display	90	-
Church, Garden Club, Welcome			Village Hall Tombola	180	-
Club, Sports Club, Village Hall,			Community Fund	1,273	35
Parish Council.					
(Each	162	22)	**TOTAL RAISED**	**2,156**	**18**

Signed:

Treasurers:

The funds raised were divided equally between St Peters Church and the Village Hall, the Welcome Club, the Garden Club and the Parish Council, for the maintenance of the play area. The remaining balance of £973.02 was retained to finance future village events.

CHAPTER 10
I REMEMBER WHEN...

By Frank Palmer

Down on Bridge

Until the late 1950s, the main meeting place for the children and young adults of the village was on the bridge, opposite the Trooper Inn. It was a common sight to see men and children of all ages, sat along the entire length of the bridge on a summer's evening. Everybody knew the place as 'down on bridge'. Often there was not enough room for everyone to sit, and the younger children would hover between the groups of young adults present, to listen to the conversation and adult humour. The topics of conservation never really changed; one's job of work, girls, risqué stories, local gossip and the catching of rabbits. There was always loud laughter, and we used to laugh along with the older men, even when we did not understand, or see the funny side of the story.

The younger children present also played various games in the street, until the arrival of the Police Constable from

Frank Palmer recalling his childhood memories down on bridge.

Stalbridge on his bicycle put a temporary halt to the proceedings. During the evening, with bedtime approaching for the younger children present, their mothers would arrive to collect them, hailing out from some distance to call them home, as they were too embarrassed to come too close for fear of some ribald comments from the young men congregated on the bridge. Football was also played in Ropers Field at the rear of the Trooper Inn. Men and boys of all age groups played until it was too dark to see the ball.

In the 1920s there were no wireless sets in the village, and on a Saturday evening, one young man would bring back an evening paper from Stalbridge, and all those present would eagerly gather around,

for the announcement of the results of the afternoon football matches. I can recall one man who attended the F.A. Cup final each year, and on the Sunday he would give a ball by ball account of the match to those assembled on the bridge. The girls passing the bridge never seemed to object to the wolf whistles that came their way, and some of the married women would engage in a little banter. I can recall one who objected to the whistles calling out 'Go back to the farmyard where you belong' There was so much natural spontaneous humour. I have never forgotten the comment of one man sitting on the bridge watching the children, including myself, on our way to Sunday School, carrying a bunch of flowering twigs from a willow tree, as it was Psalm Sunday. Where be off—faggoting ? This was the term used for tying up bundles of brushwood used for fire lighting. I was frequently envious of the young men who owned a pedal cycle and who had a few shillings of spending money in their pockets. I used to consider them extremely wealthy, especially on the occasions they decided to leave the bridge, and cycle off to Sherborne to buy some fish and chips, and in later years to attend the Picture Palace. Our village cyclists always risked a confrontation with the local police constable, due to the unreliability of either the oil, or carbide lamps on their bikes.

I fondly remember those many evenings, during the 1920s and 1930s, spent on the bridge. The humour and comradeship meant everything to us, but it really was harmless and innocent, just a bunch of local lads sitting on the bridge.

Childhood Games

We spent a lot of time in our early childhood playing games to make up for the lack of toys and our most popular game was known as Lurky, which was a form of hide and seek. Our favourite spot for playing this game was in amongst the ivy-covered ruins, near the entrance to Court Barton Field. These ruins were the remains of the former cattle pound and black-smith's shop. At the start of every game, a tin with a pebble in it would be placed on a large stone, near where the Coronation Tree now stands. The child nominated to do the seeking would wait by the stone for the others to hide; after successfully locating and touching a hidden child, they would then both race back to the stone and grab and shake the tin – the loser would be the next seeker.

Purdling was another childhood pastime, over the tubular railings alongside the brook near the Trooper Inn. Ropers Field was our favourite field in which to play, with the added attraction of the brook, and we used to catch minnows in jam jars and paddle in the water. Getting our feet wet was a sure way of finding ourselves in trouble when we arrived home, having defied our parents' instructions not to play in the water. The dried stalk of a hollow-stemmed plant was used for making a blowpipe, and a handful of ivy berries served as ammunition. Catapult elastic was hard to come by, and a strip of rubber from a discarded inner tube was used as a substitute. Boys also collected cigarette cards and enjoyed playing games with them. A player needed a deft flick to flip his card that much further than his opponent's, which gave him the right to have first go at throwing all the cards up in the air, and to keep all of them landing with the picture facing upwards. The boy who had thrown the second furthest would then do the same, and this would continue until all the cards had been won. Apart from a spinning top the only other toy I possessed was a metal hoop, made by the Stalbridge blacksmith at a cost of 9d. Cowboys and Indians was also played in Ropers Field, bean sticks and hessian sacks were carried to the field to construct the wigwams and we were armed with our crudely fashioned bows and arrows; it was here that many a Redskin bit the dust.

Other less physical games included searching for a four-leafed clover to bring us luck, and counting the bracts on a stem of Bennett grass whilst reciting the words of 'Tinker, Tailor, Soldier, Sailor' to try to foretell our future. Our cricket equipment would invariably consist of a rubber ball, six sticks cut from the hedgerow for stumps, and a bat hewn from a plank of wood. The smaller boys would find it very difficult to hold the makeshift bat upright; as for myself, I used to drop the bat and run to the other end whenever there was a possibility of run.

Ambrose Stainer collecting water from Kerr Well in the early 1930s.

Kerr Well

Before mains water came to the village, all our water had to be fetched from Kerr Well, situated in the corner of Ropers Field. Three footpaths led to the well. The one from the main street passed along the side of the garden of No. 1 Bridge Cottages, and two stiles had to be negotiated; a stone stile at the bottom of the garden, and a wooden stile near the well. We encountered many mishaps when negotiating the stiles with full buckets of water, mainly due to our careless attitude. On reaching the stile we would swing one bucket over the stile, closely followed by the other, which was being carried in the other hand. If the bucket failed to clear the stile then the contents were spilled all over us.

If mother knew that she would not be at home when we came out of school in the afternoon, then she would give us strict instructions at lunchtime to fetch some water from the well, and to fill the kettle and place it on the hob beside the fire. Often by the time we came out of school these orders had already been forgotten. As soon as mother came into view on her way home, one of us would grab the black cast-iron kettle and dash to the well to fill it up, racing back to the house before mother arrived home. The kettle was then placed on the hob in front of the fire. We were then out of immediate danger of getting into trouble, and could return to the well at a more leisurely pace with the empty bucket.

Sunday was always a busy day for the men from families who used Kerr Well as they had to fetch sufficient water for the Monday wash. Most men used yokes on their shoulders to support the two buckets which hung from crooks attached to adjustable lengths of chain. All our drinking water was stored in large earthenware pans, and the water used for washing kept in galvanised baths. Kerr Well never dried up even during the hottest of summers, and remained in daily use until the provision of a main supply to the village in 1936. The well dried up in 1954 probably due to the diverting of the spring during excavation work for the mains sewerage system.

The Outside Lav

The outside lavatory was normally located at the far end of the garden and was also known as the Little Room, or the Throne Room. When we were small children our lavatory always seemed a mile away from our house, and on dark nights we would only venture down there as a last resort, even when we had each other for company. We did not stop and study the stars during these times of emergency, and if an owl were to hoot our hair would stand on end. If the journey had to be taken on my own, then I would start whistling as I ventured out into the darkness, to try and convey to any intruder that I was not afraid, although this was far from being the case. With the mission accomplished, it was a case of head down and run back to the house as fast as my little legs would carry me, bursting through the back door, and breathing a huge sigh of relief.

Daylight hours posed a different problem; it was simply one of being able to sit on the right sized seat, for my brother had a habit of sitting on the child's seat for long periods of time, reading the squares of newsprint which served as toilet paper. If I needed to use the toilet in a hurry, I had to perch on the adult's seat, which was not very comfortable, although I did manage to avoid falling through the large hole in this seat and into the vault below. As I grew older my fear of the dark diminished, and I was able to use a candle to find the way. It was not unusual to see the flicker of a candle outside during the hours of darkness as the holder tried to shield the flame with their hand whilst wending their way down the garden path to the toilet. On a cold freezing night it was no joke to have to leave my warm bed and make my way down the garden path to the Little House, especially if suffering from constipation, which meant the stay was even longer. There could even be problems during daylight hours, due to the distance involved, especially if there was a delayed reaction to our weekly dose of syrup of figs.

It was an unpleasant task to empty the vaults and this was normally carried out on a moonlit night, with the wind in a favourable direction. With the arrival of a main sewerage system in 1954 the Little House at the bottom of the garden became obsolete, some were knocked down and the vaults filled in, and others were converted to garden sheds.

Potatoes

Potatoes were known by many names, among them spuds, taters and chiddies. The wage for a farm worker was only 30 shillings a week, with deductions of 3 shillings rent for a tied cottage, and a further 9d. for the statutory health-insurance stamp. There was not much money left to feed a family, and even less to clothe them, and for this reason many potatoes were grown. As well as the early crops grown in the cottage gardens most farm workers were allowed to grow at least one line of main crop potatoes in an arable field. Potato planting in the fields always took place on Good Friday, regardless if this day was in the early or later part of April. This was the only day available for the farm workers to carry out the planting, as Sunday was still considered a day of rest, on which only essential jobs were done. Despite some unavoidable early planting times, there was seldom any frost damage; on occasion a few would be touched by frost if they were planted in the lee of a hedge, or under the shelter of standing corn.

Potato planting in the fields followed the same routine every year – the seed potatoes were collected from the workmen's cottages by horse and putt, while the carter was preparing the horses and plough. When the first two furrows had been completed, then the chiddie dropping could start. It was not practical to drop the seed potatoes when standing in an upright position. From my own experience it was rather foolish to try and do it that way, for a knob of dirt whizzing past your ear would tell you to bend your back and do the job properly. There was an old country saying: 'One boy is a boy, two boys are worth half a boy, and three boys are worth no boy at all.' This was certainly true in our case especially when potato planting, for we had a

tendency to try to do as little as possible. When we were planting near the end of the row, with only a few spuds left in the bucket, we would plant them further apart to avoid having to walk back to the seed bag. If we were going to have some left over we would plant them closer together, to avoid having to carry them back to the start of the next row. We did not consider the fact that the evidence was bound to show when the potatoes began to shoot, so making our father aware of what we had done. When there were six of us in the family father used to reckon that it needed a ton of potatoes to see us through until the next planting season.

When the potato crop was harvested, the sacks of freshly dug potatoes were taken home by putting them through the frames of our bikes, which meant having to walk and push the cycle, though every opportunity was taken to free wheel downhill, resting our feet on the sacks. As an inducement father gave us the opportunity to pick up the remaining small potatoes to sell as pig food at a shilling a hundred weight. Having spent many hours of tedious work picking them up and carrying them towards home in the frame of the bike, an unnoticed hole in the bag left a trail of small potatoes in the road behind me. It was only when the bag became unbalanced and fell out of the cycle frame that I become aware of it. On another occasion the bag being carried in the bicycle frame of the boy in front of me burst, scattering spuds all over the road, causing him to crash headlong into the ditch. I found this very amusing, but due to the distraction it caused me, the front wheel of my bike struck one of the potatoes strewn in the road. Before I knew what was happening I had landed in the ditch alongside him.

Scrumping

Scrumping was the slang term used by children for pinching apples from the local orchards. Almost as soon as the blossom had fallen from the trees, we would become impatient waiting for the apples to grow. In fact we would start to eat them when they were little bigger than the size of a walnut, prompting mother to comment that if we did not stop gnawing away at green apples then we would get worms. Most boys were very familiar with all the orchards around the village, and the best means of entry without being detected. We also knew which trees provided the best eating apples, but we did not know the correct names of the individual species, and so we gave them our own names so that every boy knew which tree we were referring to. I can still recall some of the names, 'Good Uns', 'Good Sorts' and 'Girt Uns', to name but a few.

Some others were self explanatory, for instance an apple with a red texture running through it was known as a butcher, as we associated red with blood; should the apple be pear shaped, it was called the pear apple. One particular apple, despite being very hard to bite was nevertheless an excellent eating apple, and these were called Irons. A bitter-sweet apple that was a great favourite of ours was of a golden colour and these were known as Goldies, and Russet apples of what-ever variety were known as Rusties.

There were several different ways of scrumping; the favourite way was in daylight if there as a gap in the hedge near a tree that we knew would be loaded with good eating apples. Moonlit nights were a very good time as well, and we were able to identify the right trees by their silhouettes. Many were the hazards that came the way of the scrumper; it was all very well to crawl under some barbed wire at leisure when making an entry into an orchard, but it was a different matter when a pursuer made a quick exit more than necessary. Seldom could we afford the time to crawl back under the wire; instead we would take the option of jumping over the top. This often meant a badly scratched rear end, or a torn seat to my trousers. I remember one incident where a boy was standing on the wire, and just about to jump over to make his escape, when he overbalanced and found himself caught by the leg of his trousers and suspended upside down; needless to say he was caught on this occasion. Animals and birds could raise the alarm if we were not careful, and the barking of a dog could attract the owner's attention. Geese might also raise the alarm and we kept well clear of them. Free-range hens also provided a problem, for they would squawk incessantly.

School Days

It seems that my entire time spent at school seemed to revolve around three things; mischief, play and the cane. The most vivid memory is the visit of the school doctor. I strongly remonstrated at being stripped naked for the examination without any explanation. The next was the visit of the Nit Nurse. Pupils were formed into a line, and the nurse inspected our hair for nits, and our necks for flea bites. The most unwelcome visitor to the school was the Police Constable from Stalbridge, at which I would cast my mind back to recall any recent mischief that I had been involved in. Punishment was a subject that I was well aware of. There were some, like my brother and myself, who became hardened to it, and there were some who would show great determination not to be seen to shed a tear. There were others of course who would start to cry before the cane had reached their hand. On occasion, irate parents came to complain but they were soon sent away.

For a short while we had a temporary head who gave pupils a choice of punishment. Her preferred methods were to either send a child to stand in the corner with a book on their head, or to write lines after school. If a pupil found the boredom of writing lines or the indignity of standing in the corner to much to bear, then she would give us the choice of the cane.

The young female teacher in charge of the infants' class was a good at sketching and art work. Pupils in the senior class would swap rooms with the infants for art lessons, in the hope that it would improve our artistic abilities, and a pretty forlorn hope it was too. Senior boy pupils enjoyed these sessions, for although we were apt to misbehave, she was very reluctant to report us to the head teacher, and naturally we felt that she was a great sport. From time to time she would pause in front of a desk, and turn around a pupil's artistic achievement in order to scrutinise it more closely. On these occasions, a boy could be quite often seen on his knees under the desk, supposedly looking for a dropped rubber or pencil. On one such occasion she arrived at my desk, to find that I was missing from my seat. Suddenly I felt a stinging blow across my backside, the shock causing me to bang my head against the underside of the desk. With considerable speed I regained my seat, and turned angrily to the pupil next to me, blaming him for what had happened. I then heard the stifled laughter, and turned to see the teacher, with the ruler which she had used to dent my pride, held in one hand, and her other hand pressed against her lips trying to suppress her laughter.

Empire day, celebrated in May, was an important day in the school calendar. A Union Jack was put on display outside of the school, and inside a map of the world was pinned to the wall with the areas of the British Empire shaded in pink. On one such day, another boy and myself were sent to the store shed in the girls' playground to collect some blue ink and a small quantity of red ink. On the way back to the class-room, we noticed some white flowers growing in the border under a window. We proceeded to change them into red, white and blue, by dipping our fingers into the ink, and marking each alternate petal of the flower heads as our contribution to the day of celebration.

One certain way for a boy to find himself in serious trouble was to be caught in the girls' playground. My brother, who was nearly 14, was so absorbed in the chase, that he failed to spot the teacher until she grabbed him by the scruff of the neck. As she swung him around, one of his hobnailed boots accidentally caught her on the shin. Just before the end of the day the head teacher noticed her walking with a limp, and asked what the matter was. The young teacher refused to divulge the reason, but the headmistress persisted and reluctantly the teacher told her the truth. I knew from past experience that the best course of action was to remain silent, and not to make any excuses. We were still on the receiving end of the reprimand when one of the boys present foolishly said: "I don't for one minute think that it was anything more than just an accident." This boy was the first to have the cane, but instead of receiving it on the hand, it descended on to the seat of his trousers. As it made contact, a huge cloud of dust emerged, and floated across the classroom. Afterwards we discovered that the boy had been carrying sacks of cattle meal after school hours, without changing his clothes. This incident was to cause much humour at the poor boy's expense, and was compared to a carpet being beaten, whilst hanging on a clothes line.

Cider

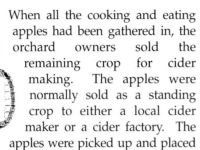

When all the cooking and eating apples had been gathered in, the orchard owners sold the remaining crop for cider making. The apples were normally sold as a standing crop to either a local cider maker or a cider factory. The apples were picked up and placed in hessian sacks, and there was an agreed rate of pay for each bag collected. The apples being sold to a factory were then transported by horse and cart to Stalbridge Station, and off-loaded into trucks at the sidings. Should the picking up operation take place over an extended period of time then the apples were stored inside a compound constructed of sheep hurdles, the problem being that there was a tendency for the apple juice to rot the bottoms of the sacks.

As boys we were often recruited to help in picking up the fallen apples and there were two methods employed for removing the apples from the trees, by either climbing the tree and shaking them off, or by using a long ash pole to knock them down. These poles were cut with a narrow tip to enable the user to flick the apples from the trees, without causing damage to the branches. Cider making was considered to be a social occasion, especially so when being carried out in the stable block at the rear of the Trooper Inn. Hurricane lamps were suspended from the rafters, and the stronger boys were given the task of turning the handle of the apple crusher – the only incentive for doing this was being allowed to drink the apple juice in the tub under the press. If a boy was foolish enough to drink too much juice then he was soon in for a rude awakening, for it tended to suddenly open the bowels, being a lot worse than a periodical dose of laxative.

The crushing machine was fitted with a tapered hopper, which allowed the apples to be gradually fed into the jaws of the crusher; the pulp resulting from this operation would be caught in a large wooden box, placed on the ground beneath it. A cheese was then prepared on the platform of the press which was built up in layers using clean straw between each layer of pulp. The straw initially overhung the sides of the platform and each layer of extruding straw was then bent over and the layer of pulp placed on top of it, which then held the cheese together. With the completed cheese now ready for pressing, a thick square board was placed on top, followed by two thick wooden blocks which were spaced equally apart, to prevent the cheese from being pushed out of shape by the descending beam of the press when the pressing operation commenced. On each side of the press a wormed metal screw rod was fitted – these ran vertically up into their respective fixed threaded sleeves, situated in the wooden overhead crossbeam. Sprocket wheels were fixed to the ends of the beam, which engaged into the wormed screws of the upright rods, and attached to them was a ratchet arrangement.

Two men were required to operate the press; standing on either side they inserted their metal tipped wooden rods into the sockets that were attached to the angled sprocket wheels. Working in unison they pulled on their respective rods, and the heavy wooden beam started to descend towards the cheese constructed on the platform below. This operation continued until the beam was exerting maximum pressure on the cheese, and the apple juice flowed out of the pulp into a trough placed beneath it. The apple juice was then transferred in to barrels, and allowed time to ferment. When fermentation was completed, the barrels were sealed with a large cork and left to mature. The barrels used for storing the cider had a capacity of several hogsheads, a hogshead being the equivalent of 50 gallons.

The pulp that remained from the pressing operation was known as pummy, and was often placed in nearby hedgerows and coppices to attract game birds. A single or double-handled cider cup was used for drinking cider in the home, but the men preferred to use a short length of cow horn when working in the fields because it was easier to carry and was unbreakable. A young lad who had just started employment was expected to carry the jar of cider out into the fields. It was also his job to serve a cup or horn full of cider to each workman, using the same drinking vessel, this task being referred to as 'doing the honours'. During this time many farmers made cider on their farms, for the provision of free cider to the workmen was an added incentive to get the work done.

Religious Activities

When we were in the choir we had to wear the same heavy boots on Sundays that were worn during the rest of the week. These boots had to be dry on Saturday night, so that they would polish up sparkling and bright for the Sunday morning service, and woe betide us if they did not. These boots were extremely noisy on the flagstone floor of the centre aisle of the church when walking from the belfry to the choir stalls. As regards our singing I am afraid that the old adage 'practise makes perfect' did not apply in our case. I suppose what was lacking in finesse was made up for by our enthusiasm. The Bishop of Salisbury was climbing into his car, after officiating at a confirmation service, when he turned to us and said that we had sung like larks. This unwarranted praise was too much for one spectator whose muttered comment suggested that we had sounded more like a nest of rooks.

Most children formed into groups at Christmas time to try to earn a few coppers carol singing, and being in the exulted position of serving as choirboys we were no exception. We decided to go further afield to try our luck, trudging through the night, and on our arrival at the large house we had targeted sang at the tops of our voices. We were anticipating a large reward and were not too concerned when nobody made an immediate appearance at the doorway. We sang with great gusto, and after a while there was some movement at the doorway. Thinking our moment had come we stopped singing. Our anticipation was further heightened when an elderly lady appeared at the doorway carrying a large handbag. She fumbled about in her bag in the darkness and handed our leader some money. As she returned inside we carried on singing, our leader felt the coins in the darkness, and then announced that she had given us three half crowns. We sang on, while one lad

struck a match to confirm that we had indeed struck it rich. Alas we were all in for a shock with the announcement that we had been given three pennies. With the stark reality of this small remuneration we broke off our singing in mid sentence and fled, for we had given more than value for money.

Hoping to recoup our losses we decided to make for an isolated farmhouse. After falling over gates and hedges and walking through a sea of mud we eventually arrived, hoping for more sympathetic treatment than we had received earlier in the evening. We had sung one carol all the way through, and we were singing the second anticipating the arrival of someone on the doorstep, when one of our party broke wind. This loud and unexpected sound set off a chain reaction of laughter amongst us, and before there was any hope of us regaining our composure the front door flew open and we were told in no uncertain terms to clear off.

When the organ blower's job became vacant I took it on at the annual salary of £1 for two services every Sunday, the reason being that we were made to attend church every Sunday, and at least now I was being paid to do so. It was also better than sitting in the choir stalls through a long boring sermon, where it was often difficult to stay awake. For in the choir stalls you were in full view of the congregation, and no matter how monotonous it became we had to try and look interested, but by blowing the organ I was behind a curtain out of sight of the congregation.

Other Memories

There was a buzz of excitement in the school classroom on hearing the news that the Fernandes family had invited us to a tea party on their lawn at Haddon Lodge. Our mother insisted on cleanliness and we were not allowed to leave the house until she had given us a thorough inspection. The pre-arranged assembly point was the Church Hut, and several adults had agreed to take charge of us as we walked to Haddon Lodge. The first part of the afternoon was spent playing games and organised sports. After tea we amused ourselves by taking it in turns to sit on a huge rocking horse. There was then more food and drink, and Mr Fernandes gave each child a packet of sweets as we walked in single file past the summerhouse window. We were then faced with the long walk home.

Miss Enid Fernandes also came to the school, and gave us a talk about her travels around the world. She showed us her collection of souvenirs, and I was especially fascinated by the spears and the bows and arrows. The following day we had to write an essay

about her experiences, and I received some unexpected praise from the headmistress for my efforts; I was thrilled to have done something right for a change.

During the winter months trapping moles gave us the opportunity of earning a little pocket money. We had been given a dozen traps by Tom Conway, a retired shepherd who had worked on Manor Farm and resided in No. 1 Bridge Cottages. Having trapped and skinned the moles, the stretched dried skins were sent off by parcel post to one of the dealers who advertised in the newspapers. With growing impatience we could hardly await for the postal order to arrive, rushing home from school to see if there was an unopened envelope on the top of the mantelpiece. We opened the envelope full of optimism, only to find that the advertised rate of 4s.6d. per dozen had been substantially reduced with an enclosed note stating that the skins were only second grade.

We were sometimes given jobs to do on the local farms, to help with the family finances, or simply to keep us out of mischief. These tasks included the clearance of stones from both arable and pastureland, digging docks in the growing corn, and weeding the kitchen garden at Manor Farm. Dock digging was paid at the rate of 3d. per 100, and stone picking 2 shillings per putt load.

During the first or second week in May the annual rook shoot would take place in a field at the top of Holt Lane, in a small area of coppice known as the Rookery. As soon as the first shots were fired, the adult birds would fly off to a distant tree, from where they would caw incessantly while the shoot was taking place. The younger lads present would collect the fallen birds and place them in a heap, and afterwards they were shared out amongst all those present. Rook pie was on many a cottager's menu the following day. Rooks are no longer to be found in the Rookery at the top of Holt Lane, the most likely explanation being that the eggs were robbed from the nests by grey squirrels.

At harvest time, with the corn being cut by the horse-drawn binder, boys would congregate in the cornfield and stand at various locations around the remaining area of standing corn awaiting the emergence of the frightened rabbits, which would then run towards the safety of the nearest hedgerow. As they ran towards us we would chase after them with a clubbed stick, hoping to catch one to take home to mother for rabbit pie the following day.

After the harvest was completed, some farmers would allow their workmen to pick up the ears of corn left scattered on the ground in the stubble field. This was known as gleaning, and it was usually the children who were expected to do this tediously boring job of work which was, however, a cheap way of keeping our hens fed during the autumn months. The corn threshing in the rick yard at Manor Farm would take place on a cold dry winter's day. The sheaves of corn were pitch forked to the top of the threshing machine, and the swirling dust would block my nostrils, causing soreness to my eyes. Every stack would be infested with a large number of rats and mice, and I would try to dispatch as many as possible with the aid of a stick.

My brother and I often used to sit side by side on the wooden toilet seats in our outside lav, puffing away at cadged cigarettes. The remaining dog ends and the box of matches would then be placed in a tin and pushed up into the thatched roof of the toilet for safe keeping. Old Mans Beard was the normal substitute for tobacco, despite the stinging sensation it gave to the tongue. Dry moss wrapped in newspaper was another method used from time to time, the smell of which was similar to that of a heap of garden waste smouldering away in a bonfire. Tea leaves wrapped in a piece of paper were not very successful, as the loose ignited particles would drop out and burn a hole in our clothing. Sometimes we used a clay pipe to try to overcome this problem, but there was a tendency for the leaves to crackle and pop in a most alarming manner.

At social gatherings in the Village Hut it was not unusual to see a group of boys huddled in a group trying to be inconspicuous as they puffed away on their cigarettes. It was at one such gathering that my brother was to encounter the Reverend Fincher's subtle disapproval of the habit. He simply engaged my brother in conversation whilst he was desperately trying to conceal the cigarette behind his back. I remember seeing the flicker of a smile on the friendly bearded face of the Reverend Fincher, as my brother began to wince with pain, trying to juggle the remains of the lighted cigarette behind his back to prevent it dropping on the floor.

Looking down the High Street from the junction of Drove Road, c.1910.

CONCLUSION

In recent years there has been a decline in the community spirit that was so evident for the most of the 20th century. The development of motorised transport, and the invention of radio, television and mass-communication systems have all played their part in this. Life has become far more stressful, and residents tend to spend their leisure hours either relaxing at home, or enjoying leisure activities away from the village. The most dramatic changes occurred in the mid 1970s. The new Village Hall project had been successfully completed, but the post-war generation of now young adults had left the village to pursue careers and greater opportunities elsewhere, leaving a large void in the social fabric of the community. The demise of the football team, closure of the village primary school, and the loss of a resident vicar hastened the decline. Membership of once thriving organisations such as the Gardening Club and the Sports Club began to decline. The Women's Institute disbanded, and the monthly dances held in the Village Hall terminated due to lack of support.

Customers at the village shop gradually disappeared leading to its inevitable closure.

Recently there has been some evidence of a reversal of this trend. The Village Open Weekends in the June of 1995 and 1996 helped to restore community spirit, and the Strawberry Fayre held in June 2000, to celebrate the arrival of the new millennium, attracted enthusiastic support from a large section of the community. The Over 60s Club, recently re-named the Welcome Club, has flourished, and a large variety of social events have taken place at the Trooper Inn since the arrival of Larry and Sue Skeats in the Autumn of 1993.

We are privileged to live in a beautiful part of Dorset, in an area unspoilt by traffic pollution, and large housing development. The millennium celebrations gave us all the opportunity to rediscover and enjoy some of the community spirit and comradeship treasured by previous generations of parishioners, and the challenge for the new Village Social Committee formed to organise this event will be to carry this forward into the new century.

Eddie Bond removing a jackdaw's nest at Brunsells Farmhouse.

SUBSCRIBERS

Ms T. L. Ashford, Battersea, London SW11

R. G. Ashford and Son

Pauline J. Baker, Stourton Caundle, Dorset

Frank, Olivia and Holli Bastable, Fourways
 Stourton Caundle, Dorset

Victoria Maud Bealing, Stourton Caundle,
 Dorset

Ruby Alice Bealing (née Bugg),
 Stourton Caundle, Dorset

Laura Beardmore (née Caddy),
 Stalbridge, Dorset

Richard James Bennett, Bishop Caundle,
 Dorset

Helen and Ben Bennett

Ken Bond, Chideock, Dorset

Brenda Broughton (née Gray),
 Stour Provost, Dorset

Samuel E. Burch, Daybrook, Cat Lane,
 Stourton Caundle, 1955–88

Rita C. Chubb (née Green),
 Shillingstone, Dorset

Mr and Mrs Rick Clarkson

Cyril E. Coffin, CBE, New Malden, Surrey

Mary Collard, Stourton Caundle, Dorset

D. B. Conduit, Stourton Caundle, Dorset

Mrs W. J. Convoy (née Guy)

Sue and Dave Cooke, Stourton Caundle, Dorset

Lt Col. and Mrs J. P. Craw, Powys Green,
 Sherborne, Dorset

Donald O. Davidge, Stalbridge, Dorset

H. M. V. and H. Dike, Stourton Caundle, Dorset

Sylvia Dunford, Dover, Kent

David B. Else, Yeovil, Somerset

Barry, Sue and Tom Evans,
 Stourton Caundle, Dorset

Mr Ken Firth, Stalbridge, Dorset

John and Christine (née Burch) Firth,
 Romsey, Hants.

Mr Raymond A. Foot, Stourton Caundle,
 Dorset

Sue and Merv Frampton, Stalbridge, Dorset

Gill and Guy Gibbons

Wayne Julian Gillam, Sherborne, Dorset

Richard Ivor Gillam, Sturminster Newton,
 Dorset

Neil and Win Gillard, Stourton Caundle, Dorset

David and Alexandra Godwin, Grange Cottage,
 Stourton Caundle, Dorset

Roslyn Goleski, Stuart, Florida, USA

Mrs Silas Gould

Mr and Mrs R. Graham, Wynway,
 Stourton Caundle, Dorset

Malcolm J. Gray, Chilthorne Domer, Somerset

Brian G. Gray, Templecombe, Somerset

Sara J. Halbard, Yew Tree Cottage

Joanna Harris, Cannington, Somerset

John Harris, Sturminster Newton, Dorset

Mr Anthony Harris, formerly of The Retreat,
 Stourton Caundle, Dorset

David Harris, Stourton Caundle, Dorset

Mr and Mrs Colin Harris, Stourton Caundle,
 Dorset

Eric T. Hayward, Templecombe, Somerset

Diana Hine (née Parsons), Stalbridge

David Hollex, Stourton Caundle,
 Dorset (1955–78)

Richard E. Hollex, Yetminster, Dorset

Richard Hollex, Stourton Caundle, Dorset

Rosemary Humphreys, Stourton Caundle,
 Dorset

Robert Husband, St Stephen, Cornwall

Fred and Joy Hutchby, Stourton Caundle,
 Dorset

Dennis Jeans, Brooke, Norfolk

Denis and Betty Jenkins, Thornford, Dorset

Lesley D. Jones, Stourton Caundle, Dorset

Bob and Jane Jones, Stalbridge, Dorset

Dr Jennifer Jones, Aberystwyth, Dyfed

Mrs E. M. Keats, Dorchester, Dorset

R. D. Knott, Templecombe, Somerset

K. John Lambert, Sturminster Newton, Dorset

Mrs Delia Lane (née Baverstock),
 Stourton Caundle, Dorset

Richard M. Loader, Wincanton, Somerset

Dr Gordon Lush, West Moors, Dorset

Mrs J. E. Maule, Middlesex

Gillian and Kenneth Moore,
 Stourton Caundle, Dorset

Ralph and Diane Mowat, Stourton Caundle,
 Dorset

A. D. and C. Mullett, Stalbridge

Mr G. and Mrs M. Mundy, Yeovil, Somerset

SUBSCRIBERS

Randolph Oliver, Bishops Caundle, Dorset
D. and A. Orchard, Stalbridge, Dorset
Eva and Brian Page, Stourton Caundle, Dorset
Michael Pain, Stalbridge, Dorset
Hugh Pain, Milborne Port, Somerset
Frank L. Palmer, Stourton Caundle, Dorset
Michael and Raine Place, Dairy House,
   Stourton Caundle, Doset
Jean Puplett (née Caddy), Sherborne, Dorset
Mrs C. J. Quinlan (née Hayward),
   Bradford Abbas
Joan L. Richardson, Stourton Caundle, Dorset
Doreen A. Ricketts (née Green), Shillingstone,
   Dorset
Olive G. Rowland,
Mr and Mrs L. Saywell,
   Stourton Caundle, Dorset
Patrick and Rosalyn Sclater, Frith,
   Stalbridge, Dorset
Doris L. Searle, Stourton Caundle, Dorset

Mrs Prudence Seddon
John and Ann Shapland and Steve Marina
Paul Shee, Poole, Dorset
Mr and Mrs John Spickernell, Oxford
Lt Col. Eddie Stocker, Stourton Caundle,
   Dorset
Margaret Stuart, formerly Okeford View
Terry Taylor, Stourton Caundle, Dorset
Christine Tucker (née Guy), Holt, Wiltshire
Cleaver Walden, Yeovil, Somerset
Ursula V. Walden, Stourton Caundle, Dorset
Peter Walden
Julia and Stuart Walker,
   Stourton Caundle, Dorset
John F. W. Walling, Newton Abbot, Devon
Nic and Linda Walters,
   Stourton Caundle, Dorset
Mrs W. Wickenden (née Walden),
   Earley, Berkshire
Mrs B. Young

ALSO AVAILABLE IN THE SERIES

The Book of Addiscombe • Various
Book of Bampton • Caroline Seward
Book of Bickington • Stuart Hands
The Book of Bickleigh • Barrie Spencer
The Book of Blandford Forum • Various
The Book of Brixham • Frank Pearce
The Parish Book of Cerne Abbas • Vale & Vale
The Book of Chagford • Ian Rice
The Book of Chittlehampton • Various
The Book of Constantine • Moore & Trethowan
The Book of Cornwood and Lutton • Various
The Book of Creech St Michael • June Small
The Book of Culmstock • Robert Garrett
The Book of Cullompton • Various
The Book of Grampound with Creed • Bane & Oliver
The Book of Hayling Island and Langstone • Rogers
The Book of Helston • Jenkin with Carter
The Book of Hemyock • Clist & Dracott
The Book of High Bickington • Avril Stone
The Book of Ilsington • Dick Wills
The Book of Lamerton • Ann Cole and Friends
Lanner, A Cornish Mining Parish • Scharron
Schwartz & Roger Parker
The Book of Loddiswell • Various
The Book of Lustleigh • Tim Hall
The Book of Manaton • Various
The Book of Meavy • Pauline Hemery
The Book of Morchard Bishop • Jeff Kingaby
Minehead with Alcombe • Binding & Stevens
The Book of North Newton • Robins & Robins
The Book of Pimperne • Compiled by Jean Coull
The Book of Plymtree • Tony Eames
The Book of Porlock • Denis Corner
Postbridge – The Heart of Dartmoor • Reg Bellamy
The Book of Priddy • Various
The Book of Rattery • Various
The Book of Southstoke • Various
South Tawton and South Zeal with Sticklepath • Roy
and Ursula Radford
The Book of Torbay • Frank Pearce
Uncle Tom Cobley and All • Stephen Woods
The Book of Watchet • Compiled by David Banks
The Book of West Huntspill • Various
Widecombe-in-the-Moor • Stephen Woods
The Book of Williton • Michael Williams
Woodbury • Roger Stokes
The Book of Woolmer Green • Various

SOME OF THE MANY FORTHCOMING TITLES

The Book of Addiscombe, Vol. II • Various
The Book of Barnstaple • Avril Stone
The Book of Bridestowe • R. Cann
The Book of Buckland Monochorum • Hemery
The Book of Carshalton • Stella Wilks
The Book of Chagford • Ian Rice
*The Book of Chittlehamholt with
Warkleigh & Satterleigh* • Richard Lethbridge
*The Book of Chittlehamholt with
The Book of Colney Heath* • Bryan Lilley
The Book of Down St Mary • Various
*The Book of Dulverton
with Brushford, Bury & Exebridge* • Various
The Book of Dunster • Hilary Binding
The Book of Hurn • Margaret Phipps
The Book of Lulworth • Rodney Legg
The Book of Markyate • Richard Hogg
The Book of Mawnan Smith • Various
The Book of Newdigate • John Callcut
The Book of Newton Abbot • Ian Rice
The Book of North Tawton • Various
The Book of Northlew with Ashbury • Various
The Book of Peter Tavy • Various
The Book of Publow with Pensford • Various
*The Book of Sampford Courtenay
with Honeychurch* • Stephanie Pouya
The Book of Staverton • Pete Lavis
The Book of Studland • Rodney Legg
The Book of Wythall • Val Lewis

For details of any of the above titles or if you are interested in writing your own community history, please contact: Community Histories Editor, Halsgrove House, Lower Moor Way, Tiverton Business Park, Tiverton, Devon EX16 6SS, England, e-mail: sales@halsgrove.com If you are particularly interested in any of the images in this volume, it may be possible to supply a copy. Please telephone 01884 243242 for details.

In order to include as many historic photographs in this volume as possible, a printed index is not included. However, the Community History Series is currently being indexed by Genuki. For further information and indexes to volumes in the series, please visit:
http://www.cs.ncl.ac.uk/genuki/DEV/indexingproject.html